on track ...

Wendy Carlos

every album, every song

Mark Marrington

sonicbondpublishing.com

Sonicbond Publishing Limited
www.sonicbondpublishing.co.uk
Email: info@sonicbondpublishing.co.uk

First Published in the United Kingdom 2024
First Published in the United States 2024

British Library Cataloguing in Publication Data:
A Catalogue record for this book is available from the British Library

Typeset in ITC Garamond Std & ITC Avant Garde Gothic
Printed and bound in England

Graphic design and typesetting: Full Moon Media

Follow us on social media:
Twitter: https://twitter.com/SonicbondP
Instagram: www.instagram.com/sonicbondpublishing_/
Facebook: www.facebook.com/SonicbondPublishing/

Linktree QR code:

Acknowledgements

I would like to thank Stephen Lambe of Sonic Bond for this opportunity to contribute to the On Track book series.

I dedicate this book to my wife, Bekah, who is responsible for some of the album cover photos contained herein, and my sons Dylan and Jacob.

on track ...
Wendy Carlos

Contents

Introduction

Mention the name Wendy Carlos and the response of the average person is to reference either *Switched-On Bach* or the soundtracks she composed for the Kubrick films *A Clockwork Orange, The Shining* or Disney's *Tron*. This is where familiarity with Carlos's output ends, however, unless you are talking to someone who has a niche interest in electronic music. My own personal journey began with her soundtrack for *A Clockwork Orange*, which I first became aware of when I learned that several of the 1980s British synth-pop bands that I had been into in my early teens, including The Human League and Heaven 17, had been profoundly influenced by Carlos's score. Ironically, this revelation occurred just as the film, long unavailable due to its withdrawal from circulation by Kubrick, had recently become accessible on VHS, meaning that my first experience of the music was in its original cinematic context. From the opening titles, it was immediately obvious to me why Carlos's work had resonated so strongly with the synth-pop bands of the 1980s – the ethereal, otherworldly sounds coaxed from her Moog (particularly the 'Music For The Funeral Of Queen Mary') were an apt and unforgettable sonic analogue to Kubrick's cold dystopian vision of 1970s Britain. Within a few weeks, I had obtained the film soundtrack (the Warner Bros version rather than the exclusive Carlos release), which, by now, had become available on CD, and then proceeded to seek out her music for *The Shining* and *Tron* (these proved significantly more difficult to acquire).

Fast forward to the mid-2000s, and after a decade's worth of university music studies, I found myself in the privileged position of teaching electronic music history and composition at Leeds College of Music. With the luxury of immersing more deeply in the subject matter, I gradually began to become aware of the full scope of Carlos's pioneering musical output, from the dazzling Moog-generated sounds of *Switched-On Bach* to the ambient New Age stylings of *Sonic Seasonings* to the groundbreaking digital synthesis experiments of *Digital Moonscapes* and the exotic tunings of *Beauty In The Beast*. However, as I navigated my way through Carlos's back catalogue (which, needless to say, involved a considerable outlay in acquiring her then-out-of-print LPs), I quickly realised that there was very little information available about her music beyond her own liner notes (which were often richly detailed) and the few interviews that I was then able to access. This necessitated my own in-depth research into the recordings, exploring the often classically influenced musical content and learning about the technological influences that made the music sound the way it did. More than a decade later, the situation of wider research into Carlos's work remained much the same, with the exception of a recent biography published in 2020, which shed new light on Carlos's personal life, including the gender-related issues with which most people are familiar. However, this still left a considerable gap where the music was concerned, prompting the idea that I might usefully be able to address the situation by turning ten years' worth of teaching notes on Carlos's recordings into a practical guide for the interested listener.

What To Expect From This Book

This book surveys all the Wendy Carlos albums released between 1968 and 1998, from *Switched-On Bach* to *Tales Of Heaven And Hell*, including the much sought-after 1980 soundtrack for the Kubrick film *The Shining*, which, despite featuring only two of her pieces, is generally regarded as a seminal Carlos LP. I have also included two additional sections at the end of the book, one entitled 'Miscellaneous Releases, Compilations And Curiosities', which covers a number of other recordings Carlos has been associated with, including one-off production projects with third parties and miscellaneous compilations, which do not strictly qualify as dedicated album entities. The other section, 'Carlos Re-Released', deals with the now coveted remastered editions of Carlos's work released by East Side Digital (ESD) between 1998-2004, mainly to highlight bonus material and other significant changes, including new artwork and liner notes, which the reader might find useful to know about.

As we progress, the circumstances of the creation of each album will be outlined, followed by a track-by-track analysis in which I will highlight many different aspects of the music. I should point out that unlike the artists featured in most of the books in the *On Track* series, the bulk of Carlos's output is instrumental rather than vocal in nature; hence, we are not going to be dealing very often with lyrics here. Also, the focus of much of Carlos's work, at least in the first decade of her career, is on arranging *other people's* music for the synthesizer, with a strong bias towards classical music (popular music only features occasionally, such as on the album *By Request*, for example). In writing this book, I'm therefore assuming that its readership is likely to have an interest in classical music, its composers and the kinds of musical genres they were writing in (e.g. symphonies, sonatas, suites, etc.) – indeed, you would probably not be drawn to Carlos's work if you didn't. Furthermore, while the later part of Carlos's career after the completion of *Switched-On Brandenburgs* in 1980 is more about her own composing activity, this is, again, strongly influenced by classical music aesthetics, which are the foundation of her musical outlook. This means that if we are to fully appreciate the nature of the material that Carlos is working with and how it influences her creativity, we cannot avoid talking about classical musical concepts and using certain musical terminology as we progress. However, just as the best classical music programme notes are designed to put across ideas about the music in an easily understandable fashion, I have likewise endeavoured to keep my explanations straightforward and accessible. It should be added, incidentally, that throughout her career, Carlos regularly provided her own detailed liner notes to accompany her recordings, suggesting that she expected her listeners to engage with such terminology and to listen to her music attentively rather than passively.

Central to Carlos's recorded output is, of course, music technology, including the various incarnations of the synthesizer she was involved with during her career, from the analogue Moog of the 1960s and 1970s to the digital GDS and Synergy devices of the 1980s, and finally, the computer-based sampling and synthesis tools of the 1990s. While I will, therefore, be frequently referring to aspects of Carlos's musical gear, I don't intend this to be overly technical, but rather, I will be talking about her use of technology as an aspect of her creative vision. There will also be some focus on the non-musical concepts expressed in the album artwork and liner notes on recordings such as *Sonic Seasonings* and the post-1980s LPs – *Digital Moonscapes, Beauty In The Beast* and *Tales Of Heaven And Hell* – which form an important part of the listening experience and amplify the musical content. Together, these various perspectives will give us a broad context for appreciating the influences and processes behind Carlos's innovative music.

Readers of this book who are already devoted fans of Carlos's work will be aware that copious information on all her recordings can be found on her website, much of which mirrors the content of the expanded liner notes and enhanced CD material that she provided for the ESD re-releases. Her website also offers many other valuable documents, including numerous articles and reviews which are highly recommended reading. While I have naturally had to rely upon some of this material to clarify key facts, I have endeavoured to go beyond this, delving into the archives to locate additional historical perspectives and critical commentary to enrich the narrative, the aim being to create a wide-ranging and informative picture of how Carlos's work has been received and discussed over the decades.

Finally, while some *On Track* books have included glossaries to assist those who are not too familiar with music theory, I have instead opted to provide brief explanations of certain musical terms as they are encountered, which the reader can then refer back to if necessary. In some cases, the reader will also encounter timings (expressed in the format 0:00), which are intended to help identify important elements and navigate some of the more complex musical structures while listening.

Biography

Before diving into the recordings themselves, I would like to offer a brief overview of Carlos's career to establish some context for our discussions. While numerous Carlos biographies can be found online, the details in these can often be ambiguous and, in some cases, inaccurate, a common problem with internet sources where word-of-mouth style copying and pasting is the norm. For this reason, most of the factual information presented here about Carlos's early life and career has been drawn from 'hard copy' material that can be regarded as trustworthy, such as music industry commentary (e.g. *Billboard* magazine), album liner notes, reliable books and various interviews that Carlos has given over the years in publications such as *Keyboard* magazine, whose content is verifiably from the horse's mouth.

Wendy Carlos was born in Pawtucket, in the state of Rhode Island (New England), on 14 November 1939. She was initially trained as a classical musician, receiving lessons in piano from around age six and, in keeping with US classical music tastes of the 1940s and 1950s, learned to perform the 19th-century Romantic repertoire (composers such as Chopin and Liszt). She was later to rebel against this training in her gravitation towards 18th-century Baroque music and the works of Bach, as well as progressive 20th-century composers, including Stravinsky and Ravel. Interestingly, at the same time, Carlos was given tuition in popular music theory and began to compose, notably writing a 'Trio For The Clarinet, Accordion And Piano' – the choice of instrumentation suggests a fusion of classical and popular perspectives. Alongside her musical activities, Carlos also began to show a keen interest in science and technology, like many hobbyists, engaging in experimental tinkering with electronic equipment in her parents' basement. Such was her aptitude for electronics that, by the age of 14, she had built a computer (for which she was awarded a Westinghouse Science Fair grant) and, by the age of 15, had constructed a non-equal tempered keyboard, a device which anticipated her later explorations of altered tunings on albums such as *Beauty In The Beast* and *Switched-On Bach 2000*. Carlos's gravitation towards music technology was unsurprisingly reflected in her growing enthusiasm for electronic music, specifically the *musique concrete* works of French composer Pierre Henry, whose pieces often combined conventional music with manipulated 'found' sounds recorded from the natural environment.

From 1958-1962, Carlos continued to pursue her musical and scientific interests as a student at the prestigious Brown University, Rhode Island, majoring in Music with a Physics minor, during which time she further honed her skills as a composer. Then from 1962-65, she undertook graduate work at the Columbia-Princeton Electronic Music Center under the tutelage of Otto Leuning and Vladimir Ussachevsky. This was particularly important for Carlos's development, familiarising her with the cutting-edge techniques of contemporary avant-garde electronic music and the technologies used to make it. From these studies emerged her earliest acknowledged pieces in the electronic music genre, two of which – the 'Variations For Flute And Electronic Sound' and the 'Dialogues For Piano And Two Loudspeakers' – appeared on the 1965 compilation LP *Electronic Music*. After her graduation from Columbia-Princeton, Carlos spent three years as an engineer at New York's Gotham Recording Studios, where she met Robert B. Schwartz, a fellow engineer who assisted her in building a specified home studio in the living room of her small West End Avenue apartment. This established a model of independent home-based music production that Carlos was to replicate in two further set-ups during the 1970s and 1980s, the 'brownstone' studio in Manhattan and the loft studio in Greenwich Village.

The most prescient partnerships formed during this period were with synthesizer pioneer Robert Moog and producer Rachel Elkind. Carlos first encountered Moog at Audio Engineering Society gatherings around 1964/5, and thereafter, began to work with him on evolving and perfecting the revolutionary Moog 900 series modular synthesizer, the instrument on which she would develop her unique electronic classical music aesthetic. Moog was receptive to Carlos's advice, at her request, making two important improvements to his prototype – the addition of touch sensitivity and portamento control – which significantly increased the synthesizer's potential for expressive musical performance. Carlos's timing was fortuitous in that the synthesizer was, through Moog's innovations, finally beginning to reach a form that made it recognisable to musicians as a useable music performance tool. Earlier devices, such as the RCA Mark I Synthesizer housed at Columbia-Princeton, for example, had been unwieldy machines which occupied entire rooms, boasted hundreds of controls and were unintuitive to communicate with musically. With the advent of solid-state technology, Moog was able to resolve these issues of practicality by greatly reducing the synthesizer's size and, perhaps most importantly, incorporating a keyboard.

Carlos's association with Elkind, which lasted from *Switched-On Bach* to her score for *The Shining* in 1980, was also of vital importance in shaping her musical aesthetic. Elkind, an able musician who specialised in singing, had begun her career as a secretary to Columbia Records president Goddard Lieberson, a valuable connection which later enabled her to broker a deal for the release of *Switched-On Bach*. By 1968, she had set herself up as a producer and teamed up with Carlos to form Trans-Electronic Music Productions Inc (TEMPI), the organisation which came to represent the pair's unique brand of synthesizer-based electronic music. Elkind was pivotal in influencing Carlos to move away from her more abstract mid-1960s electronic style to focus on perfecting her classical synthesizer arrangements on the Moog, resulting in the album's worth of material that became the million-selling *Switched-On Bach*, released by CBS in late 1968.

The unexpected success of *Switched-On Bach* catapulted Carlos into the public eye as both a pioneer of electronic music and a symbol of the synthesizer, which, due to her efforts, was now becoming widely regarded as a bona fide musical instrument. Carlos immediately capitalised on this frenzy of interest with an innovative follow-up LP, *The Well-Tempered Synthesizer* (1969), which further refined the techniques showcased on *Switched-On Bach*, including an early attempt at voice synthesis. This record likewise dominated the *Billboard* Classical charts, ironically only being kept off the top spot by *Switched-On Bach* itself. During this same period, her extraordinary film soundtrack for *A Clockwork Orange* and the proto-ambient concept album *Sonic Seasonings*, both released in 1972, also began to elevate her profile as a composer of original music. While *A Clockwork Orange* took Carlos's classical arranging/composing style into darker and (with 'Timesteps') rather more abstract territory, *Sonic Seasonings* brought back to the surface her interests in progressive electronic music and *musique concrete*. A further Bach-focused LP, *Switched-On Bach II*, appeared in 1973 with a programme that, despite showcasing a close emulation of Carlos's approach on the first album, again resulted in sales figures suggesting that the public had not yet tired of her formula. By contrast, 1975's *By Request* was a hybrid of musical perspectives in which she further refined her synthesizer arranging aesthetic while flexing her compositional muscles on elaborate quasi-classical tracks like 'Pompous Circumstances'. In 1979, Carlos began work on her penultimate Bach-focused recording, *Switched-On Brandenburgs* (released in 1980), which featured all six of Bach's Concertos cast in a broad spectrum of tone colours that appeared to signal the peak of her accomplishments in the field of analogue synthesis. 1980 also saw the short-lived release of the soundtrack for the film *The Shining*. Although it used only a small amount of Carlos's music, the soundtrack further cemented her reputation as a pioneering electronic composer. Ironically, these last two projects marked the end of her collaboration with Elkind, as well as the conclusion of the 'analogue' period of her Moog-dominated synthesizer work.

The early 1980s saw a dramatic change in Carlos's sound as she began to embrace emerging digital synthesis technologies, her new sonic signature first being showcased on the 1982 soundtrack for the Disney film *Tron*. In a metaphor of the film's own pioneering CGI-meets-live-action visuals, her score merged the familiar sound of her Moog with the unique tones of the GDS digital additive synthesizer, together with a full orchestra, to dramatic effect. This was also the decade that saw the full emergence of Carlos's composer personality on two ground-breaking recordings: *Digital Moonscapes* (1984) and *Beauty In The Beast* (1986). Like *Sonic Seasonings*, both were concept albums whose subject matter – planetary moons and world music cultures – gave rise to some fascinating musical and sonic explorations, each based in the sound world of her constantly evolving digital orchestral sound library (named the LSI Philharmonic) and (on *Beauty In The Beast*) a fascination with exploring alternative tuning systems. By this point, the Moog had been almost completely retired, although it would surface again briefly in the early 1990s. *Digital Moonscapes* and *Beauty In The Beast*, while generally well received by the critics, were more of an acquired taste for the wider Carlos fanbase, although both later earned a cult following. However, the next two albums – *Peter And The Wolf/Carnival Of The Animals – Part II* (1988) and *Switched-On Bach 2000* (1992) – saw Carlos reconnecting with her classical music arranging and composing roots, both achieving respectable placings in the *Billboard* Crossover and Classical Album charts.

From the mid-1980s, Carlos began to make occasional recordings for smaller independent labels, such as Audion and Telarc, her contract with CBS coming to an end in 1987. However, in 1998, she was offered a longer-term recording deal with the Minneapolis-based East Side Digital label (ESD), with whom she released her last major album, *Tales Of Heaven And Hell*, a reflective, quasi-religious musical meditation on the afterlife. The remainder of her time with ESD was spent remastering the bulk of her back catalogue (the master rights had, by now, reverted to her) in high-definition 20-bit audio format, providing fans with a heightened digital listening experience commensurate with the era of the CD. Her last release for the label, the two-volume film music compilation *Rediscovering Lost Scores* (2005), thus far appears to have been her final musical statement to her public.

NB. Although Carlos had been living as a woman, Wendy Carlos, since the late 1960s, the first five albums (from *Switched-On Bach* to *By Request*) discussed in this book were released under her birth name, Walter. Thus, the original LP versions of these records will carry this name, while any post-1980s re-releases of the same recordings will be found under the name Wendy. Also, any reviews and advertisements quoted that refer to Carlos's recordings in the earlier period will typically use her birth identity.

Switched-On Bach (1968)

Personnel:
Wendy Carlos: Moog synthesizer, performance, arranging and engineering
Rachel Elkind: producer
Benjamin Folkman: musical adviser
Record label: Columbia Records MS 7194
Format: LP (stereo and mono versions)
Recorded at West End Avenue, New York
Release date: October 1968
Highest chart position: US: 1 (*Billboard* Classical LPs), 10 (*Billboard* 200)
Running time: 39:45

Switched-On Bach is among the most successful classical music recordings of all time and one of the very few in the classical genre to sell more than a million copies during the initial period of its release (the album was certified gold in the US in August 1969 and continued to chart for another five years, achieving platinum status in 1974). It remains the defining work of Carlos's career, making her a household name and a seminal influence on countless composers and performers who had come of age in the 1960s, including Giorgio Moroder, Stevie Wonder and Rick Wakeman. A decade on and the album's influence was still being felt in the work of synthesizer aficionados, including British synth-pop pioneers of the 1980s who held Carlos up as an icon of musical futurism, a reputation clinched by her seminal work on the soundtrack for the 1971 film *A Clockwork Orange*.

On the surface, the LP appears to be little more than a collection of Johann Sebastian Bach (1685-1750) favourites, including 'Air On A G String', 'Jesu, Joy Of Man's Desiring', 'Wachet Auf' and the popular Brandenburg Concerto No. 3, which would not seem out of place on a typical bargain-bin 'best of Bach' compilation disk. What made the album so distinctive, surprising and even shocking at the time, however, was not the music (great though it is), but rather its electronic realisation and presentation. The key ingredient here was the Moog synthesizer, which Carlos employed in a highly imaginative and exploratory manner to re-invent Bach's orchestrations. In doing so, she evolved a palette of tone colours unique to the new technology, which have since remained inextricably associated with the synthesizer aesthetic. A second important factor was Carlos's approach to recording the album, using multitrack techniques, a commonplace in the popular music sphere but one which flew in the face of classical music norms. This arose from the constraints of the Moog, a monophonic rather than polyphonic instrument (that is, it only allowed for the performance of a single melodic line, no chords), requiring Carlos to record Bach's pieces 'additively' one layer (or even one note) at a time, painstakingly assembling each musical thread in isolation on her eight-track Ampex, a process which occupied many months. She also mixed the music down in a way that did not necessarily reflect a traditional acoustic setting, resulting in an in-your-face sound which was worlds away from the 'natural balance' of high-fidelity classical recordings of the period. It was this quality that no doubt prompted the critic Hubert Howe (in *Perspectives Of New Music*) to describe the album as 'a dazzling, slick, plastic-coated Madison Avenue commercial product'. With *Switched-On Bach*, we are, therefore, in the territory of a classical music recording that could never have resulted from a live performance at all, whether in terms of its sonic characteristics or its physical execution.

Switched-On Bach was also prescient in another way in that it foreshadowed the significant changes in the structure of the music industry that were going to come about as a result of increasing technological democratisation. Carlos created the album in her own private studio on West End Avenue in New York using a multi-track tape machine, which she had constructed herself using Ampex components. An independent set-up like this had few parallels at the time (the producer Joe Meek and the inventor-musician Les Paul are among the more well-known pioneers of what is today known as the 'DIY' producer type) and effectively pre-empted the era of what Brian Eno was later to refer to as the 'studio as a compositional tool'. The most important consequence of Carlos's independence from the commercial studio environment was that she was able to take the necessary time to develop her vision for re-imagining Bach's music on the synthesizer, something which would not have been feasible had she been subject to studio schedules and expenses. The project also foreshadowed a new model of the producer-artist relationship, which focused on collaboration rather than top-down hierarchical dictation. Carlos worked closely on the album with friend and producer Rachel Elkind, who had steered the project towards Bach's music in the first place, recognising its potential as a vehicle for a new synthesizer aesthetic.

Switched-On Bach was widely discussed and debated at the time of its release, much of the commentary being focused on whether the LP qualified as a 'classical' music recording. On the one hand, the fact that the LP received three Grammys in 1969 – Best Classical Album, Best Classical Performance and Best Engineered Classical Recording – suggested that Carlos's achievement was to be taken seriously in these terms, a position which was also reflected in the remarks of some classical musicians. For example, Canadian classical pianist Glenn Gould, who had ironically abandoned a concert career to pursue the ideal recorded performance in the studio, pronounced *Switched-On Bach*, in *Saturday Night* magazine, December 1968, to be 'the record of the year (no, let's go all the way – the decade)!' For some purists, however, Carlos's radical use of the new technological medium placed the recording at a certain distance from the performance traditions of classical music, eliciting some irate responses. Charles Fager, in a review in *The Christian Century*, December 1969, commented that 'None of the performances on the album sounds better – or even as good as –

solid instrumental versions of the same pieces', comparing playing Bach on the synthesizer to 'building a Baroque cathedral out of styrofoam'. Donal Henahan's otherwise more positive *New York Times* review in November 1968 expressed concern that the music's technical difficulties were being overcome by machines, thereby removing the aesthetic pleasure derived from witnessing human virtuosity in action (he thus failed to appreciate how much performance there actually was on the album).

Perhaps most surprisingly, *Switched-On Bach* was regarded with suspicion by electronic musicians, who felt that re-imagining classical masterpieces on the synthesizer was an inappropriate use of the new technology. Harold C. Schonberg's comment, in his 1969 *New York Times* review of the album, that what 'composers of electronic music should be doing is creating their own kind of music' encapsulates the majority verdict here, with critic David Ernst even going so far as to suggest that the album didn't qualify as electronic music at all. These were perhaps not unfounded reservations when considering that the initial response to *Switched-On Bach*'s immense success was a plethora of imitations, in which almost all forms of music, from nursery rhymes to contemporary pop hits, were touched by the hand of Moog (among the more successful efforts were Gershon Kingsley's *Music To Moog By* and Gyl Trythall's *Country Moog: Switched-On Nashville*). In these terms, *Switched-On Bach* was a retrogressive step which debased the synthesizer and associated it with 'non-serious' easy-listening music. Having said that, it was the ivory tower mentality of the electronic music community that had, up until now, prevented the sounds of the synthesizer from reaching beyond a small group of aficionados in the first place. As Gene Lees wrote in his lengthy feature review for *High Fidelity* magazine in December 1968, 'Carlos ... has already made a considerable contribution, perhaps the major one to date, to the popularisation of the synthesizer as a legitimate musical instrument rather than a laboratory toy for specialists or a bloop-bleep maker for science-fiction movies'.

While these various concerns reflected the uneasiness of the musical establishment at the implications of Carlos's recording for the future of musical performance and composition, it is important to remember that *Switched-On Bach* was also an album that managed to enter the *Billboard* 200 Pop chart and climb as high as the top ten. In other words, the recording appeared to have just as much relevance to the popular music audience, a consumer group well-accustomed to technologically mediated musical novelty and generally more accepting of genre-bending experimentation. Ultimately, Carlos's decision to use Bach's music was an innovative and elegant means of bridging the divide between the two camps and the album was pivotal in introducing the synthesizer to the ears of the mainstream public in a way which connected it firmly to recognisable notions of music. Carlos also succeeded in reinventing Bach for a younger generation, reaffirming his greatness in a new technologically modernised setting, which, like many past 'transcriptions' of the composer's work, offered a new way of hearing the music. As Robert Moog observed in his comments on the album's sleeve notes: 'Carlos ... has shown that the medium of electronic music is eminently suited to the realisation of much traditional music, and in doing so, has firmly brought the electronic medium into the historical mainstream of music.'

A final comment relates to the album artwork, which exists in two versions. The original 1968 release showed Bach in a comical 'mugging' stance in front of the Moog synthesizer. The choice of this sleeve related to the marketing context within which *Switched-On Bach* was intended to be sold, namely Columbia's 'Bach-to-Rock' campaign, which aimed to capitalise on the growing interest of rock groups in using elements of Baroque music in their work (for example, Procol Harum on 'A Whiter Shade Of Pale'). In an attempt to connect with the youth consumer group that Columbia imagined to be interested in such music, the decision was made to give Bach an informal, accessible appearance – making him 'down with the kids' as it were. However, not only was this image considered trivialising by Carlos, of both the music and the Moog itself, it was also badly reproduced. Subsequent appeals to the president of Columbia Records, Goddard Lieberson, were sympathetically received, leading to a reissue of the LP with an updated image from the same Horn/Griner photo sessions, which now presented Bach in a much more dignified pose.

Sinfonia To Cantata No. 29 (3:20)

One of Bach's most exuberant masterpieces, the Sinfonia is the perfect opener for the LP, showcasing both Carlos's technical virtuosity and the precision coordination she was able to achieve within the limits of the multitrack tape-recording technology available to her. The music will probably be familiar to most listeners in its original version for violin as the Prelude To The Partita For Violin In E (BWV 1006). However, Carlos's arrangement is based on a re-working of the piece for the orchestral Sinfonia Of Cantata (BWV 29), 'Wir Danken Dir, Gott' (composed in 1731), scored for organ, brass, woodwind and strings, making this, in her words, 'a transcription of a transcription'. Carlos's synthesizer version offers a distinctive and colourful re-imagining of the original orchestration presented in a crisp, bright-sounding production, which brings the intricate details of Bach's music sharply into focus. As with much of the LP, Carlos's approach combines approximations of the sounds of the Baroque orchestra (particularly brass and winds) with timbres unique to the electronic medium.

'Air On A G String' (2:27)

Probably the most famous of all Bach's pieces, the 'Air On A G String' has been covered by numerous performers in a wide range of musical contexts, one of the best-known examples being Jacques Loussier's 1966 version for a jazz trio, which later gained popularity in the UK on account of its use in the long-running series of 'Hamlet' cigar adverts. The piece originally began life as the slow movement of Bach's Orchestral Suite No. 3 in D major (BWV 1068), the title 'Air On A G String' later being appended by 19th-century violinist August Wilhelmj, who re-arranged the music so that the main lyrical melody line could be played on the violin's lowest string. Carlos's moderately paced version draws on Bach's original orchestral score but reimagined as a woodwind-like quartet; the melody, placed in the high register, is treated with a tone that resembles an oboe (the realisation is dedicated to French oboist Marcel Tabuteau, who died in 1966). Among other things, Carlos's performance demonstrates the level of expressive playing she was able to coax from the Moog at this time, such as her use of vibrato on the long held notes (that is, the effect of causing the pitch to waver slightly).

Two-Part Invention In F Major (0:40)
With the first of the three 'Two-Part Inventions' included on this disc, Carlos now moves to a more stripped-back two-line texture. The *Inventions And Sinfonias* (dating from around 1723), from which these works are taken, are economically conceived keyboard pieces intended by Bach to assist in learning the instrument, as well as developing compositional awareness. Naturally, the reduced number of parts leaves the synthesizer more exposed, placing a greater onus upon Carlos to develop distinctive and varied tone colours. She also uses the spatial technique of placing individual musical lines in different parts of the stereo field (using headphones helps one to appreciate this when listening), something that would not of course have been possible with a single keyboard instrument. The first Invention, No. 8 In F Major, was one of Carlos's earliest choices of material for the LP and dates back to her time as a student at the Columbia-Princeton Electronic Music Center. It is based on arpeggios, or broken chord textures (widely spaced intervals which outline each chord structure), a style which lends itself well to a synthesizer treatment, as it enables a range of timbres (i.e. tone colours) to be explored across the octaves.

Two-Part Invention In B-Flat Major (1:30)
In his sleeve notes for the album, Benjamin Folkman comments upon the 'extraordinary ingenuity of the stretto' in this Invention (No. 14). Essentially, what you are listening for here (towards the end of the piece from 1:10) is the piling up of the leading theme, with each entry occurring in quick succession, thereby heightening the tension of the music. The softer, more 'rounded' tones created by Carlos for the melodic lines (based on sine and triangle waves) produce a mellow effect, a more distorted character becoming apparent with the onset of the stretto.

Two-Part Invention In D Minor (0:55)
An interesting aspect of this Invention (No. 4) is the 'classic' squelchy (sawtooth) tone of the synthesizer voice heard in the right-hand speaker.

Also, listen out for the distinctive voice that enters in the left speaker in the last few seconds of the piece (around 0:38), which is given a more distanced spatial treatment using a reverb effect. Carlos's use of these kinds of production techniques serves as a reminder of the relatively artificial nature of these realisations when compared with traditional classical music recording practice.

'Jesu, Joy Of Man's Desiring' (2:56)

Another very well-known Bach piece, excerpted from Cantata (BWV 147) (1723), this graceful, melodic number had long been saturating the airwaves by the time Carlos came to realise it in 1968. Indeed, in her remarks for the 1992 reworking of the track for *Switched-On Bach 2000*, Carlos recalls that she herself had known the piece since childhood when it had been used 'to close the broadcasting day for one of my favourite FM stations'. Reflecting the more emotional side of a composer whose work is often associated with the cerebral and mathematical, it is certainly well placed to contrast with the Inventions. The most interesting aspect of this realisation is the unusual timbre employed for the counter-melody (first appearing at 0:20), which employs a tuned white noise waveform (Carlos has discussed the process of realising this track in her commentary 'Initial Experiments', which appears on the *Switched-On* Box Set ESD re-release). Critic Gene Lees, in *High Fidelity*, December 1968, wrote (using her birth gender) that 'Carlos has so humanised the synthesizer that he manages to make 'Jesu, Joy Of Man's Desiring' sentimental, and it's the one track on the album I dislike'. Praise indeed for a pioneer of what, in some quarters, was still regarded as little more than 'machine' music!

Prelude And Fugue No. 7 In E-Flat Major (From Book 1 Of The Well-Tempered Clavier) (7:07)

The two pieces heard next on the LP are taken from the first volume of Bach's most acclaimed collection of works for keyboard, *The Well-Tempered Clavier*, comprising 48 Preludes and Fugues in total. In this music, Bach explores the fugue, an intellectual form in which a principal musical theme, called the 'subject', and an accompanying 'counter-subject' are presented in a variety of different musical guises (here, the synthesizer plays an important role in distinguishing these ideas from one another), the Preludes serving to set the mood in each case. Perhaps the main pleasure (for the attentive listener) is in trying to keep track of these various musical lines through to the end of the piece. This music, incidentally, was originally composed to be played on the harpsichord, a comparatively monochrome instrument, with the synthesizer offering considerably more colouristic potential.

There is a regal quality to Carlos's sound design for Prelude No. 7, which is clearly intended to evoke the qualities of a brass ensemble, resulting in sonic atmospheres, not unlike those that Vangelis was later to make famous in his

soundtracks for the films *Bladerunner* and *Chariots Of Fire*. This weighty
approach certainly suits the 'titanic cumulative effect' of the music that
Folkman identifies in his album liner notes. The Fugue itself is, by contrast,
lighter and more nimble in character, the tones possessing an almost metallic
quality, sometimes reminiscent of steel drums.

Prelude And Fugue No. 2 In C Minor (From Book 1 Of The Well-Tempered Clavier) (2:43)

This popular *moto perpetuo* prelude (meaning based around a continuous
repeated pattern) is given a highly individual distorted timbral setting
by Carlos, culminating at 1:00 in a dramatic improvisatory flourish. The
peculiarity of Carlos's approach gave *Gramophone* critic John Gilbert, in
April 1969, cause to wonder 'if one's equipment had not developed a buzz'.
A relatively reverberant treatment is also apparent here, which gives the track
a larger-than-life sound. In a similar manner to Prelude No. 7, the timbres of
the dance-like fugue have a clipped, staccato quality, with the richly toned
bass line being especially Moog-ish in character.

Chorale Prelude 'Wachet Auf' (3:37)

Another popular melody of Bach, taken from his Cantata No.140, 'Wachet
Auf, Ruft Uns Die Stimme', also known as 'Sleepers Wake'. The piece is
perhaps best known as the Chorale Prelude for organ (BWV 645), comprising
three musical lines – the low bass, the mid-range Chorale (an old hymn
tune, not composed by Bach) and the decorative high melody (composed
by Bach). The music receives a straightforward and subdued treatment from
Carlos, which emulates organ style, each element being given a distinctive
timbre which remains consistent throughout the piece, with no additional ear
candy to speak of. While perhaps a little bland in the context of the whole, it
provides a suitable point of repose before the LP's concluding act.

Brandenburg Concerto No. 3 In G Major – First Movement (6:35)

For the finale of the album, Carlos and Elkind chose to undertake an
ambitious realisation of Bach's third Brandenburg concerto, a work originally
comprising two movements, each of a length and formal complexity that
demanded a rather more elaborate strategy for their synthetic orchestration
than the miniatures that make up the bulk of the LP. The Brandenburg
Concertos (there are six in all, composed during the years c. 1718-1721) are
regarded as one of the high peaks of Bach's output, not to mention classical
music in general. To subject one of them to a rendering on the synthesizer
was clearly a bold decision, guaranteed to provoke a response from the
classical music critics, particularly where the more experimental elements of
its (newly composed) slow middle movement were concerned.

The First Movement was originally scored for a string ensemble split into
three small groups – three violins, three violas and three cellos – and uses

what is known as a *ritornello* form, in which a main section featuring the 'big tune' returns at periodic intervals, at which point, the string sections play together as a group (usually referred to as the *tutti*). This is contrasted with passages where the instrumental sections play solo, thereby (as observed in the earlier discussion of the Inventions) creating a situation of exposure which demanded an imaginative sonic treatment. Bach has also constructed the movement to include many instances of call and response between instruments, affording an opportunity for some interesting tone painting. As expected, Carlos does not limit herself to Bach's original string instrumentation in her sound design, incorporating a wide range of often otherworldly timbres that are unique to the synthesizer. Consider, for example, the variety of tone-colour contrasts that she employs in the remarkable passage between 5:00-5:20, in which a melodic idea is passed around the various sections as it gradually moves down into the bass register.

Brandenburg Concerto No. 3 In G Major – Second Movement (2:50)
Carlos's realisation of the Second Movement of the Concerto was by far the most adventurous on the LP, not least because the music is an original composition in *cadenza* style conceived to flesh out the two solitary chords that bridge the existing movements in Bach's original score. Add to this Carlos's highly imaginative electronic treatment of this new material and you have one of the most outlandish renderings of Bach imaginable. For the uninitiated, a *cadenza* is an extended section of music that was traditionally improvised (in other words, composed on the spot), one of the few moments when a classical performer is allowed to be spontaneously creative (in comparison to popular music). This is a challenge because it requires an experienced composer who is also well-versed in stylistic pastiche to be able to produce something that fits with the musical idiom. Carlos's solution in this instance was to create what she calls a 'flamboyant fantasia' using, according to Benjamin Folkman, ideas from Bach's Chromatic Fantasy And Fugue In D minor (BWV 903) and the Great Fantasia And Fugue For Organ In G Minor (BWV 542); in other words, interpolating quotations from two other Bach pieces that were deemed suitable. More provocatively, however, Carlos also undertook a certain amount of electronic experimentation with the sounds themselves, using techniques gleaned from her earlier experiences working at the Columbia-Princeton Electronic Music Center. The result is a highly amusing send-up of avant-garde electronic music cliches highlighting, more than any other track on the album, the advanced technological context within which she is working. Of Carlos's efforts, *High Fidelity* critic Gene Lees wrote that Carlos...

...has thrown in a lot of whacky electronic effects, glissando swishes and windy whistlings, a pong-pong like a struck pie-pan and a sound that is an odd cross of bird twitterings and water running over stones. I find the track hilarious, but if you object to humour in music, you are going to be mightily offended by it.

Critic Eric Salzman also singled out the movement for special comment in his somewhat tongue-in-cheek review of the album in *Stereo Review*, comparing Carlos to Leopold Stokowski, a conductor renowned for his progressive attitude to classical record production:

> But the triumph here in this box full of Bach is undoubtedly the Third Brandenburg Concerto with its yummy electronic-Stokowski orchestration, its superbly comic use of vibrato and its side-splitting, chromatic-electronic, kiddie-kartoon kadenza interpolated between the two outer movements. Go-for-Baroque, motor Baroque, Stokowski-Baroque, pseudo-electronic hokum, total confusion of the medium and the message – it is not often that one finds a record that so devastatingly satirises so much all at once.

Brandenburg Concerto No. 3 In G Major – Third Movement (5:05)
With the final movement, Carlos lets loose with the fireworks in a scintillating and energetic realisation, which, in marked contrast to the First Movement, is built predominantly from bright, crisp-sounding synthesizer timbres, which flash by at considerable speed. One is reminded at times of the sound of a 19th-century mechanical organ of the type commonly found in fairgrounds, rather like the one electronically manipulated to great effect by George Martin on The Beatles' 'Being For The Benefit Of Mr Kite'. As it was physically impossible to play the movement live at its actual required tempo on the Moog keyboard as it then existed, Carlos recorded the music at half speed at one octave below standard pitch, the tape then being sped up to produce the correct pitch. Hence, we have a unique example of a studio-based problem-solving strategy being deployed to achieve the desired musical effect. As with the First Movement, the range of colours Carlos manages to conjure from the Moog synthesizer throughout the piece is remarkable, the effect being further enhanced once again by her approach to stereo placing and her imaginative use of reverb.

The Well-Tempered Synthesizer (1969)

Personnel:
Wendy Carlos: Moog synthesizer, performance, arranging and engineering
Rachel Elkind: producer
Thomas Frost: producer
Record label: Columbia Records MS 7286
Format: LP
Recorded at West End Avenue, New York
Release date: November 1969
Highest chart position: US: 2 (*Billboard* Classical LPs), 199 (*Billboard* 200)
Running time: 37:58

At first glance, *The Well-Tempered Synthesizer* (subtitled 'More Virtuoso Electronic Performances Of Bach, Monteverdi, Scarlatti, Handel') appears to be a product of the 'we need a follow-up' syndrome that always occurs when a record label realises it has a runaway hit on its hands. Certainly, this might be suggested by the speed at which the new LP appeared; in technical terms, it is a remarkable feat given the previously discussed complexities of recording classical music using the Moog synthesizer at this time. The advertising blurb (published in *Stereo Review*, November 1969) that accompanied the release, with its tongue-in-cheek goading of the classical critics, also implied that the new formula Carlos had discovered for presenting classical music was far from being exhausted:

> 'The synthesizer ain't got no pizzicato. Not even a vibrato', the classicists said. And so they laughed when Walter Carlos wanted to play Bach on it. But they stopped laughing. Fast. And by the time he got to Handel, Scarlatti, Monteverdi and more Bach on his new Columbia album, *The Well-Tempered Synthesizer*, the classicists weren't so classical anymore. They had learned that the beauty of their music is that it can change, grow and become so renewed that every generation can love it. Of course, that knowledge cost them a little. But they're trying to sit down and live with it. And if the men who make music in their lives can do it, it's only because, pizzicato or no pizzicato, they know a good thing when they hear it. And so will you.

In its innovations with the electronic medium, however, which arose from a problem-solving spirit motivated by a desire to further explore the possibilities of the synthesizer for realising classical music, the recording is some distance from being merely a cash-in. As the LP's sleeve notes indicated, on *The Well-Tempered Synthesizer*, Carlos and Elkind self-consciously aimed to move beyond *Switched-On Bach* into new territory; in Elkind's words, carrying 'the maturation of the medium another step forward'. In programming the material for the new LP, contrary to the title's suggestion (an obvious play on Bach's *Well-Tempered Clavier*), Carlos clearly did not wish to remain focused only on Bach; hence, the bewigged composer is now in the esteemed company of his most important German contemporary, George Frideric Handel (1685-1759), as well as two major Italian Baroque composers, Claudio Monteverdi (1567-1643) and Domenico Scarlatti (1685-1757). Only one of Bach's works appears on the LP, albeit a substantial one, the Brandenburg Concerto No. 4, whose realisation is certainly one of the disc's stand-out moments. This was not merely repertoire chosen for the purposes of providing a more varied programme, however, but also music that offered new arranging challenges, ultimately giving rise to new production strategies (particularly Carlos's 'hocketing' technique) that would form an important part of her musical aesthetic thereafter.

The Well-Tempered Synthesizer was, on the whole, well-received by the critics, who, while raising eyebrows at the LP's more outlandish experiments in the Monteverdi 'Domine Ad Adjuvandum' (see below), were stunned and delighted by Carlos's technical achievements, which appeared to outweigh any concerns with purism where the electronic medium was concerned. Especially significant was the endorsement of Carlos's work by the musical cognoscenti in Britain's esteemed classical recordings publication *Gramophone* in March 1970:

Ever since this disc has been in the house, it's hardly been off the turntable, and all my friends (yes, record reviewers do have friends, whatever you may have thought) have gone through the same sequence of reactions as I. First, astonishment that this machine – I don't know quite how it works and am not sure I'd understand if I were told – can produce so enormous a range of timbres, some almost exactly resembling the orthodox colours of flute, harpsichord, cornett, etc., some evocative, some entirely original and patently electronic ... Then sheer admiration for the quite incredible ingenuity of it all: the precise calculation of ictus, duration and decay of every note, the choice and range of tone-colours, the expert orchestration (knowing exactly when to add in an initial 'chuff' as from a 2-foot organ flue, or to pick out just a note or two as by a xylophone), the well-adjusted dynamic levels of the various musical lines, the artistic phrasing. Above all, the excellent taste of most of it: hats off to Walter Carlos!

NB. A few short test tones are heard on the original LP (also included at the end of the ESD re-release) prior to the opening Monteverdi track. This was commonplace on recordings of an audiophile nature at this time and had the purpose of giving the discerning listener a reference point for calibrating their stereo speaker system.

'Orfeo' Suite: Toccata; Ritornello I; Choro II; Ritornello II; Choro II; Ritornello II (3:15) (Claudio Monteverdi)
The 'Suite' that opens the LP is a medley of short dance-like pieces taken from Claudio Monteverdi's influential early Baroque opera *L'Orfeo* (1607),

which takes as its theme the myth of Orpheus, who descended into the underworld to retrieve (unsuccessfully as it turned out) his deceased bride Eurydice. Orpheus, it should also be added, was associated with uncommon musical prowess, his playing renowned for its ability to tame the wild beasts, a not inappropriate metaphor, perhaps, for Carlos's interactions with the synthesizer! The Suite's short opening Toccata is probably one of the most famous fanfares in the Baroque repertoire, and like the dances that follow it, it features an imitative style of writing in which a melody in one voice is immediately repeated in another. Thus, as we observed with *Switched-On Bach*, we have multi-layered music of a character that demands a certain resourcefulness in the creation of synthesizer sounds that will bear repeated hearing. Carlos's sleeve notes indicate that she aimed (and in the Monteverdi 'Domine Ad Adjuvandum' which concludes the LP) to 'suggest rather heraldic, resonant sonorities', a reference perhaps to the brass and wind-like sounds that feature prominently.

Sonata In G Major, L. 209/K. 455 (1:38) (Domenico Scarlatti)
The four Scarlatti Sonatas on the LP mark a return to keyboard repertoire which, as observed in Carlos's treatment of the Two-Part Inventions on *Switched-On Bach*, brings forth some imaginative (and, as it happens, rather un-keyboard-like) sonic experimentation. Together with the Monteverdi 'Domine Ad Adjuvandum', the Sonatas have been the most discussed of this LP's selections, mainly on account of Carlos's innovative use of the 'hocketing' technique. For our purposes, a simple working definition of hocket, taken from the Collins *Encyclopedia Of Music*, is as follows:

> The breaking up of a melody into single notes or very short phrases by means of rests, particularly as used by composers and discussed by theorists in the 13th and 14th centuries ... Most often, it is used in two parts at a time so that one sings while the other has a rest.

To fully do justice to the subject of hocketing would ideally require a book in itself, but this definition is enough to help us understand in basic terms what Carlos is aiming for in her arrangements. In a 1979 interview with Dominic Milano for *Contemporary Keyboard* magazine, Carlos explained why she had decided to take this approach with the Scarlatti pieces:

> The Scarlatti Sonatas on the *Well-Tempered Synthesizer* were the first instances of deliberate, self-conscious use of high degrees of hocketing or pointillism. It came about because of the stark original music, which was often nothing but one note in the left hand and one note in the right hand. What do you do to flesh that out? Do you play something that sounds very dull on a monophonic instrument? No, what you play is ya-dah-dah-dah on one track, and on the other, dah dah-dah-dah. It sounds like you're stuttering,

almost, when you do them one at a time, but if you're lucky, or if your intuition's right when you're laying this out – trying to figure out what notes you're going to do in any one colour – the totality does interlock together.

Hence, what you are listening for in all four of the Scarlatti pieces is the constantly shifting tone colour created by the fragmentation of the musical phrases, at times even occurring on every other note, an effect which is further heightened by the placement of the sounds within the stereo image (headphones are advised to appreciate the strategy). Note that Carlos also uses the word 'pointillism' in her description, which is a reference to the painting style popularised by French artists in the late 19th century, particularly Georges Seurat, in which a vibrant image is created through the amassing of minuscule dots of colour on a canvas. As with Seurat's pictures, Carlos's arrangements can be appreciated either by focusing on the specific details of sound colour as they occur or by taking in the total musical effect.

Carlos first introduces the hocketing technique in the lightning-fast first Sonata (in G Major), showcasing its potential with considerable panache. Scarlatti's original keyboard version comprises a simple two-part texture characterised by a continuous flow of notes in the right hand accompanied by a simple bass in the left. In Carlos's treatment, this now springs to life in a dizzying array of alternating tone colours, the pronounced stereophonic call-and-answer effect as the line is segmented and flipped between the two speakers, making for an exhilarating listening experience.

Sonata In D Major, L. 164/ K. 491 (3:50) (Domenico Scarlatti)
In her sleeve notes, Carlos states that the D Major Sonata was the first Scarlatti piece arranged for the LP, which may explain its more reserved treatment in comparison to the previous number. The piece is far from uninteresting from a sonic perspective, however. The tone colour shifts, which appear to sound from a distant space at 0:32 and 1:49, produce a marvellous effect. Carlos also carefully varies the timbre of the repeats for the Sonata's main A section (compare 0:00 with 1:16), while the unrepeated B section's progress from a subdued staccato timbre to a glorious sparkling sunlight is highly dramatic.

Water Music (George Frideric Handel)
Bach's exact contemporary, George Frideric Handel, was one of the most versatile and commercially successful composers of the Baroque era, the bulk of his career being closely associated with England, where he settled in 1712. The 'Water Music' (composed around 1715) is a collection of three suites of various lengths for orchestra written at the request of George I for performance in a royal procession on the River Thames. Carlos chose to realise three of the work's most familiar movements in a generally straightforward fashion.

Bourrée (0:43)
A short and snappy number. The bourrée is a brisk French dance dating from the early 17th century which has a feeling of two beats to the bar. The piece is in binary form, meaning it has an A and B section, both of which are repeated, giving Carlos the opportunity to employ a contrasting tone colour on each occasion.

Air (2:42)
The Air, whose melody is certainly as iconic as Bach's 'Air On A G String', is a lyrical piece which Carlos treats to an emotive, almost vocal-like, timbral setting, giving a hint of what is to come in the LP's concluding Monteverdi arrangement.

Allegro Deciso (2:57)
The upbeat Allegro features brass and woodwind-like timbres in alternation, thereby giving an appropriate nod to the regality of the original scoring. Also, listen out for the emulated timpani rolls that occasionally punctuate the music. The second, more reserved contrasting section (from 1:02) has tones that are, at times, suggestive of the pipe organ.

Sonata In E Major, L. 430/K. 531 (1:52) (Domenico Scarlatti)
The next two Scarlatti pieces contain further hocketing experiments, Carlos commenting in her liner notes that the E Major Sonata is 'perhaps the most elaborate example of such fragmentation' and an exemplar of 'the type of coloristic and stereophonic rapid shifting that is so idiomatic to and effective in the electronic music media'. In terms of its sound world, Carlos's setting is certainly, at times, reminiscent of the experimental electronic whimsy we encountered in the second movement of the Brandenburg Concerto No. 3. Once again, we are treated to an appealing stereophonic extravaganza and a wide variety of synthesizer tones, including the prominent use of white noise at the piece's conclusion between 0:24-0:32.

Sonata In D Major, L. 465/K. 96 (2:25) (Domenico Scarlatti)
A slick treatment, with the hocketing again very much in evidence, accompanied by some strongly contrasting colour fluctuations. This final Scarlatti Sonata of the quartet appears as a summation of Carlos's virtuoso sound design skills thus far, the section towards the end of the piece showcasing a delightful range of timbral juxtapositions.

Brandenburg Concerto No. 4 In G Major, BWV 1049 (Johann Sebastian Bach)
Side two of the LP begins with Carlos's second foray into the world of Bach's Brandenburg Concertos, this time focusing on the popular No. 4. This piece has a different instrumentation to the Third Concerto, with the solo

parts now being taken by two recorders (Carlos refers to these as flutes in her sleeve notes) and one violin, which is pitted against an accompanying string orchestra with harpsichord. The musical content here also differs from the third Concerto, including extended sections of solo material and imitative writing, which presents opportunities for a fascinating array of tone-colour contrasts. Meanwhile, the larger-than-life studio production, including the use of Carlos's 'hybrid echo-reverberation techniques', brings the music's innermost details to the fore. Those familiar with the more conservatively distanced aesthetic of the traditionally recorded Brandenburgs will undoubtedly find this an exhilarating listening experience. Carlos's achievement in realising this Concerto drew a gushing endorsement on the album cover from Canadian pianist Glenn Gould: 'Carlos's realisation of the Fourth Brandenburg Concerto is, to put it bluntly, the finest performance of any of the Brandenburgs – live, canned or intuited – I've ever heard.'

I – Allegro (8:03)
The lengthy dance-like first movement (in a fast 3/8 time) contains a substantial first *ritornello* section featuring some flashy writing for the solo violin part. The violin (which in Carlos's rendition sounds far from violin-like) becomes particularly busy from its solo entrance at 1:31, at which point, we hear the left/right speaker hocketing technique we encountered in the Scarlatti Sonatas, later breaking into a continuous stream of fast 32nd notes (in both sections, the hocket effect occurs at one bar intervals, that is, every three beats). In comparison to the unorthodox violin tone, Carlos's flute timbres are, in her words, 'realistic/imitative', emulating the old-fashioned wooden recorder with which listeners would have been familiar from period-observant performances of the Brandenburg Concertos (Carlos remarks in her sleeve notes that, at times, she is also trying to suggest the modern transverse flute and the piccolo). It is worth noting, incidentally, that while it is straightforward to produce basic flute tones on a synthesizer, it is more challenging to emulate performer nuances, such as the effect of the player's breath as it passes through the tube and the tonal modulation introduced to bring sustained notes to life. Ultimately, however, while this and the other instrument patches created by Carlos might stand on their own terms as individually authentic, when they are heard together in combination, the resulting sound world is unique to the synthesizer.

II – Andante (3:30)
In the slower Andante movement, the violin is decidedly less busy, functioning either as a bass line to the two recorders or doubling the accompaniment. Overall, the musical texture is more homogenous, the instrumental parts moving together in rhythmic unison, with few diversions into solo material (the brief flourish that concludes the movement is the exception). As before, Carlos's realisation is far from being a mere imitation,

however, and the sounds presented here, while sometimes suggestive of familiar instruments (including the brass family), occupy their own reality. Among the standout sonic features are the quirky filter-shaped timbre allotted to the recorders (characterised by the momentary 'wisp' at the start of each note), which is reiterated (perhaps to saturation point) throughout, the bright trumpet-like timbre used for the violin part, the distorted character of the bass and the clangourous echoed metallic chord at the end.

III – Presto (4:40)

This high-spirited movement (given a blisteringly fast rendering in Carlos's version) is a sophisticated construction which combines virtuosic concerto-like sections with rigorous contrapuntal writing of the type encountered in the fugues on *Switched-On Bach*. The latter can be heard from the outset with the multipart entries of the main theme which builds to a climax. This then gives way to a concerto-like passage, which reduces the focus to the three solo instruments before resuming the ensemble fugal style. Virtuosic elements then reappear in the violin part, which, like the first movement, gradually increases its rate of rhythmic activity, initially based on 8th notes before moving to rapid 16th notes, each section again being treated using Carlos's now-familiar hocketing style. There is plenty of intricate detail in this piece to support Carlos's sound design ambitions, the fugal aspects being well articulated using staccato (short) timbres, which are a key characteristic of the movement. Once again, the two recorder parts have distinguishable wind-like qualities, while the sounds allotted to the solo violin appear nothing like their namesake.

'Domine Ad Adjuvandum' From 1610 Vespers (2:13) (Claudio Monteverdi)

The *Vespers*, which can be counted amongst Monteverdi's greatest musical achievements, are settings for a choir of evening prayers sung in Latin to celebrate the feast of the Virgin Mary, which were usually accompanied by brass, wind and stringed instruments. It will be immediately noticed in listening to this piece that the music for this particular text, 'Domine Ad Adjuvandum', happens to be based on the fanfare-like Toccata we heard at the beginning of the LP, thereby providing a fitting recapitulation to the proceedings. Presented with the question of how to deal with the voices, Carlos decided to undertake a rather more radical realisation than she had previously attempted with the technological resources available to her. In the liner notes for the original LP release, Carlos states that her realisation 'represents a first-order experiment in crossing the gap between vocal and instrumental media, and it contains some of the most complex sounds I have obtained on the present synthesizer'. In essence, what we have here is an early example of voice synthesis, painstakingly achieved via the use of multiple synthesizer modules and a carefully coordinated performance using hands and feet 'to select pitch, vibrato, loudness, portamento and two vowel-producing resonances' for the six choral voices. As it turned out, this was a unique strategy that was not repeated, Carlos subsequently adopting (on her 1971 soundtrack for *A Clockwork Orange*) a specially built vocoder for her ensuing forays into vocal synthesis.

Naturally, reviewers singled out Carlos's attempt to emulate the human voice for special focus, anticipating the probable reaction from the purists. *New York Times* reviewer Donal Henahan, for example, wrote in October 1969 that the disc has...

...hold it, now – a simulacrum of human voices, synthesized on Carlos's own expanded and exfoliated version of the Moog. The experiment lasts only a few moments, in an excerpt from Monteverdi's *Vespers For The Blessed Virgin Mary* (1610), but there it is, and the audacity of it all is sure to infuriate some listeners for whom the synthesizer and sin are, at the moment, interchangeable terms.

For the most part, however, commentators tended to regard Carlos's vocal realisation as an attempt at a musical joke. In March 1970, The *Gramophone*, for example, referred to the 'hilarity at the wicked satire on consonant-less, distant choral singing (in the Monteverdi *Vespers*)', while in *High Fidelity* in February 1970, Leonard Marcus wrote:

I was terribly amused by the last band [the word 'band' here referring to an individual LP track], the Monteverdi 'Domine Ad Adjuvandum', with its attempt at portraying solo and ensemble singers through electronic manipulation. I presume that I was amused for the correct reason, namely the poor vocal enunciation. A marvellous satire. I couldn't understand a word.

A Clockwork Orange (1972)

Personnel:
Wendy Carlos: Moog synthesizer, performance and arranging
Rachel Elkind: producer, vocals on 'March From A Clockwork Orange'
Record label: CBS S 73059
Format: LP
Recorded at Elkind 'Brownstone' Studio, West 87th St, Manhattan
Release date: 1972
Highest chart position: US: 4 (*Billboard* Classical LPs), 146 (*Billboard* 200)
Running time: 41:37

Carlos's score for the 1971 Stanley Kubrick film *A Clockwork Orange*, based on the book by Anthony Burgess, is without doubt one of her most iconic and widely known works. It is among the earliest film scores to feature the synthesizer prominently and in a manner that perfectly complements the film's narrative and cinematography, offering a potent mix of sound and vision that was to resonate strongly with British and European electronic musicians in the 1970s. The soundtrack for *A Clockwork Orange* reached the public's ears via two official LP editions, one released by Warner Bros (K46127) in 1971, which was marketed as a direct tie-in to the film, and one by Columbia (CBS S 73059) in 1972, which was billed as Carlos's exclusive 'complete original score'. It is the Columbia edition that is the focus of the track-by-track analysis below, which differs substantially from the Warner Bros LP. For example, on the Warner Bros version, Carlos's music rubs shoulders with the various conventional classical recordings and popular songs that Kubrick had sourced for the film, such as Rossini's famous 'La Gazza Ladra' and Gene Kelly's rendition of 'Singin' In The Rain'. While complete versions of Carlos's synthesizer arrangements of the second and fourth movements of Ludwig Van Beethoven's Ninth Symphony are also included, her most important original contribution, 'Timesteps', was heavily cut from its epic length of 13:50 to a paltry 5:10 as a reflection of Kubrick's partial use of the music in the notorious 'Ludovico treatment' scenes. This was thankfully rectified on the Columbia release, on which the full version of the piece now takes centre stage as the LP's opening track.

The liner notes to the Columbia release tell an interesting story about the music's conception and creation. They show that Carlos had already begun to work on the Beethoven material and 'Timesteps' prior to becoming involved with Kubrick's film. She had selected the fourth movement of Beethoven's Ninth Symphony primarily due to its substantial choral part, which offered a vehicle for further exploration of the synthesised vocal techniques introduced on *The Well-Tempered Synthesizer*. 'Timesteps', a more abstract and experimental electronic piece, was conceived as introductory music to be placed prior to the Beethoven movement, in Carlos's words, 'to ease the listener into this new sound of a well-known piece'. However, she recalls

31

that not long after she had begun to compose 'Timesteps', she was given a copy of Burgess's *A Clockwork Orange*, which subsequently exerted a strong influence on its musical direction.

It was only after completing these early projects that Carlos and Elkind became aware that Kubrick was in the process of filming Burgess's book, and this led them to pitch the pieces for potential inclusion in the soundtrack. The decision could not have been more prescient, with Carlos's choice of Beethoven being particularly apt for a film whose chief protagonist, Alex, is obsessed with the composer and references his music repeatedly. Kubrick secured Carlos and Elkind's agreement to use the material, after which the pair proceeded to record further tracks, including a synthesizer arrangement of Rossini's 'La Gazza Ladra' and an original composition, 'Country Lane'. While both were ultimately rejected for the film, they are featured on the later Columbia LP, where they give a sense of how a complete Carlos score might have sounded had the director been more amenable. As Carlos has noted in her sleeve notes to *Rediscovering Lost Scores* 1 & 2 (released in 2005), Kubrick tended to become attached to music used provisionally during the 'spotting' process (when pre-existing pieces are tested out against the film prior to commissioning original music), leading him to dismiss new material created after the fact. It is arguable that in this case, however, Kubrick's choice to keep certain conventional recordings and juxtapose these with Carlos's modern synthesizer versions adds something to the psychological atmosphere of the film. The appropriateness of the synthesizer to the film's plot is summed up by critic Alexander Walker in his 1972 book *Stanley Kubrick Directs*:

> In *A Clockwork Orange,* one must be equally aware of the musical concept he [Kubrick] elaborates. It is hardly accidental, for example, in a film where the hero's behavioural processes are systematically destroyed and re-created in another form, that the music, which plays an integral part in such 'remedial' therapy, should itself have been strained through the Moog synthesizer by the composer.

Whereas the programming of the Warner Bros release unsurprisingly reflects the general sequence of events in the film, Carlos is clearly thinking of the Columbia version as an album experience. Her decision to place 'Timesteps' at the beginning is a bold one, given the music's unorthodox character, and serves to suggest that this recording, like Burgess's book and Kubrick's film, is likely to be far from a conventional experience. The various classical arrangements which make up the bulk of the soundtrack material are sandwiched between 'Timesteps' and the concluding track 'Country Lane', which likewise offers a more abstract musical experience. Carlos's music for *A Clockwork Orange* was realised in Rachel Elkind's 'brownstone' studio on the Upper West Side of Manhattan, New York.

'Timesteps' (13:50) (Carlos)

While the continued focus on producing electronic arrangements of classical music indicates that *A Clockwork Orange* can be seen as being, for the most part, a further outgrowth of *Switched-On Bach* and *The Well-Tempered Synthesizer*, 'Timesteps' is a track that signals the emergence of a musical style that is more reflective of Carlos the composer, anticipating the direction she was to take on *Sonic Seasonings* (released in the same year as the Columbia version of the soundtrack). 'Timesteps' is a long and complex piece, very much in the tradition of the experimental electronic music movement that Carlos had engaged with in her earlier work and revisited in a somewhat jocular fashion on *Switched-On Bach*'s Brandenburg Concerto No. 3, Second Movement. The piece can also be appreciated in the light of the more 'mainstream' *musique concrete* experiments that had already taken place in the popular music arena in the music of such bands as The Beatles, on 'Revolution No. 9' (1968), and Frank Zappa, on recordings such as *Freak Out* (1966) and *Lumpy Gravy* (1968). Interestingly 'Timesteps' appears to have garnered something of a cult status on its release, particularly with students, for whom it was a favourite request on US college radio stations during the early 1970s.

'Timesteps' does not operate like a conventional piece of music, its structure coming across on the whole as free-form, although there are recurrent snippets of melody, chord progressions, occasional regular rhythmic patterns and other identifiable 'found' sounds (ticking clocks, for example) that give it an overall unity. It may assist the listener to keep in mind Carlos's comment that the music aims to capture the 'feeling of the opening scenes' of Burgess's book, which, as those familiar with both the novel and the film will recall, narrate the catalogue of 'ultra violence' perpetrated by Alex and his Droogs on unsuspecting members of the public. In this light, the music certainly has something of a feeling of ominous threat about it, although there are, at the same time, contrasting moments of considerable calm and serene beauty. However, it is not strictly necessary to listen for a narrative and it can be just as rewarding to let the events of this impressive musical soundscape simply wash over you.

The following is a listening map of the music's main highlights:

An ominous, distorted, delay-effected synthesizer tone leads into a gradually intensifying build-up of squealing pipe sounds (Middle Eastern bagpipes spring to mind) over chimes, ultimately leading to a climactic chordal resolution. Out of this emerges a brief snippet of 'Music For The Funeral Of Queen Mary', the film's opening title theme.

Unsettling electronic atmospherics, permeated by distant church (perhaps Gregorian) style chanting of 'Hosanna In Excelsis'. The choir is synthetic, created using Carlos's vocoder (see later in regard to the Beethoven 'March').

The music begins to gather pace as repetitive, percussive rhythmic patterns accompany a distinctive Moog bass line melody, this section appearing to function as a kind of introduction to a livelier, higher-pitched theme, the phrases of which ricochet between the speakers.

More experimental electronic atmospherics, amidst which we hear ticking sounds (perhaps intended to be suggestive of the machine-like 'clockwork' orange). Wisps of synthetic vocal material. A darker atmosphere intrudes and a variety of intriguing sounds (Carlos's score states 'glass bells' and 'tremulant effects') are heard swamped in cavernous reverb. More chanting of 'Hosanna In Excelsis' before the squealing pipe-like sounds reappear, the music building to a second dramatic chordal resolution.

Momentarily, we appear to be in a 'natural' environmental setting. Chirping crickets are subsumed into a passage of aggressive 'tribal' drumming, over which a variation of the primitive Middle Eastern pipe melody is heard (does this aim to suggest the Droogs engaging in a rumble with the rival gang in the abandoned theatre, perhaps?). This segues into a curious dream sequence, with effects of waves crashing/wind and seagull sounds, and a beautiful chorale-like melody is heard off in the distance over chimes.

A new section of complex polyphonic music (suggesting an influence of the fugue) appears, in which multiple strands of synthesized melody begin to overlap one another, the phrases increasing in their rhythmic rapidity before running out of steam. Ticking sounds precede another section of synthetic choral music, culminating in loud, explosion-like crashes (the Moog's white noise is apparent here).

The final part of the piece comprises a densely textured segment of 'aleatoric' music built from overlaid repeating percussive patterns, electronically generated timbres, synthesized vocal textures and fragments of the pipe music, the latter once again becoming a central focus. After reaching a final climactic chord (one that we have heard twice before), the piece concludes with a few isolated dabs of sound.

'March From A Clockwork Orange' (7:00) (Ludwig Van Beethoven)

In keeping with Carlos's original aims, the Beethoven arrangement which follows appears to emerge quite naturally from 'Timesteps', having the effect of concentrating the preceding chaos into something more concrete and directed. The word 'March' does not accurately describe the music here, though, as the piece actually comprises a more substantial section of the later part of the fourth movement of the composer's Ninth 'Choral' Symphony, during which the choir is introduced to dramatic effect in a performance of the famous setting of Friedrich Schiller's 'Ode To Joy'. The March itself, which is in a Turkish style, enters after a brief pause from around the 2:31 mark and serves as both a diversion (re-working the main tune) and a tension builder. This is then followed (at 4:10) by an exhilarating fugato – i.e. truncated fugue – section (Beethoven was strongly influenced by Bach at this point in his life), which culminates in the choir's re-entry with the 'Ode To Joy' theme at 5:54.

The Ninth is regarded as Beethoven's crowning musical achievement, whose music, in combination with Schiller's poem, has been interpreted as a profound statement of joy and hope for the brotherhood of mankind. However, in the context of the film, it gains a rather sinister resonance when placed against the footage of Nazis shown to Alex at the peak of the 'Ludovico treatment' sequence, causing his mental breakdown. This alienating effect is reflected in Carlos's music, which, already in a synthetic orchestral guise, includes voice tones (reciting texts kept in the original German) that are generated using a vocoder, a device (invented by Homer Dudley in 1938) which enables the analysis of speech signals and the mapping of the resultant sonic fingerprint to a sound source so that the words can be pitched. In Carlos's case, the vocoder was a 10-band device built for her by Robert Moog in 1970 (which she refers to as a 'Spectrum-Encoder-Decoder'), and the output sound source is her synthesizer. The recitation of the text itself was undertaken by Rachel Elkind, hence it is her voice that you hear 'singing' on the recording. It is hard to overstate how strange this re-working would have appeared to the cinema audiences at the time, given that the original Beethoven version would have been widely known (and loved) in its traditional setting. Interviewed in *Melody Maker* in 1972, Elkind commented, 'We played it to friends, and they were somehow terrified. Here was a machine trying to sound like a human and getting so close. It was just like HAL all over again.'

'Title Music From A Clockwork Orange' (2:21) (Carlos/Elkind/Henry Purcell)
This piece, which is arguably the most iconic music of the soundtrack, is used at the beginning of the film to introduce the main character and, thus, appears at the head of the Warner Bros release. On the Columbia LP, however, it is placed after the Beethoven piece, creating a rather subduing effect relative to what has just been heard. As it happens, we have already heard a tiny fragment of the theme, which is taken from 'Music For The Funeral Of Queen Mary' (by England's most famous Baroque composer, Henry Purcell (1659-1695)) in 'Timesteps' (at 1:15), although it would be hard to spot this without knowing the tune already.

Purcell's grave and stately processional sets the mood perfectly, Carlos's treatment of the music's opening synthesizer chord having a remarkable effect as it emerges from the ether (using tape speed manipulation) into full definition, depositing us into the cold artificial reality of the world inhabited by the character of Alex, whose menacing visage is subsequently revealed in close-up. Discussing her approach to arranging the piece, Carlos commented in an interview with Vincent LoBrutto that 'The Purcell is transmogrified into something more spacy, electronic, weird, and it worked. Stanley liked it very much and he never looked back.' Another key musical moment to listen for is the foreboding 'Dies Irae' theme, which enters at 1:07, an ancient church melody that will be instantly recognisable to anyone who knows Carlos's score for *The Shining* (or alternatively, anyone who knows Carlos's inspiration for its use – Hector Berlioz's *Symphonie Fantastique*, Fifth Movement). Here, we have one of many examples of Carlos's penchant for transplanting themes from one musical context into another, a practice which we will encounter repeatedly as we survey her recordings.

'La Gazza Ladra' (5:50) (Gioachino Rossini)
'La Gazza Ladra' (the Italian translation of the 'The Thieving Magpie') is a synthesizer arrangement of the famous overture to the opera of that name by Gioachino Rossini (1792-1868). It will be recalled that this music, in its original orchestral guise, is used as an accompaniment to one of the film's most disturbing assault scenes, which takes place in an abandoned theatre before dissolving into an almost balletically choreographed gang fight. Carlos's arrangement appears to have been an afterthought rather than one specially conceived for use in the film ('As we would have done it, had there been time'). Her sound design strategy here is, on the whole, straightforwardly imitative in that, often, what we hear are timbres that suggest string, brass and wind instruments quite convincingly. Elsewhere, though, we have passages where the instrumentation is quite unexpected, such as the section from 2:33-2:52, in which the tone colours appear to suggest an accordion.

'Theme From A Clockwork Orange (Beethoviana)' (1:44) (Carlos/ Elkind/Henry Purcell)
This short diverting piece reprises 'Music For The Funeral Of Queen Mary', but now with a decidedly different musical character. Gone is the stateliness of the original, and instead, we have the main melody re-worked in a slow, lyrical style accompanied by a flowing triplet pattern reminiscent of the opening movement of Beethoven's 'Moonlight' Sonata (this is the probable reason for the bracketed subtitle 'Beethoviana'). The synthesizer timbres are simple and imitative in conception – a flute/whistle-like sound for the main tune and metallic, chiming timbres in the chordal backing.

'Ninth Symphony: Second Movement' (4:52) (Ludwig Van Beethoven)
Carlos's second Beethoven setting is an abridged arrangement of the Second Movement (the Scherzo) of the Ninth Symphony. A Scherzo (literally meaning 'a joke') is a multi-sectioned musical form, typically in three beats to the bar and played very fast. A key driver of the excitement in this particular Scherzo is Beethoven's use of the fugato, in which four distinct voices (spread across the orchestra) are introduced gradually, eventually coalescing into loud percussive chords, and finally, a dance-like passage. The second half of this edited arrangement (from 2:30) focuses on the Trio section, which is in a contrasting duple (2 beat) time signature. As with Carlos's rendering

of the 'The Thieving Magpie', her synthesizer realisation is generally quite conventional in its approximations to recognisable instrument types, maintaining a uniform balance of sonorities and avoiding overt colouristic experimentation. Of the various sounds heard here, the synthesized timpani, which appears prominently in the fugato section, are especially realistic, while the Trio section affords an opportunity to hear the instrumental sonorities in relative isolation, allowing one to appreciate the level of authenticity Carlos achieves, particularly with the brass and winds.

In the film, Carlos's version of the piece (which appears alongside standard orchestral versions of the music) is employed as a sonic weapon by Alex's captors to torture him for his earlier crimes against them, causing him to attempt suicide (unsuccessfully) from the window of the bedroom in which he is being held prisoner (hence the title 'Suicide Scherzo' on the Warner Bros version of the soundtrack). At 4.52, the version of the Scherzo that appears on the CBS release is significantly longer than the Warner Bros edit, which clocks in at only 3.07.

'William Tell Overture' (1:17) (Gioachino Rossini)
Taken from 'The March Of The Swiss Soldiers' section of Rossini's Overture, this is another famous piece that is so seared into the public's imagination (many audiences of this era were familiar with the music's use in the *Lone Ranger* TV series, as well as Looney Tunes cartoons) that it could only be given a fresh life through a synthesizer rendering. The blistering speed at which the piece rushes by scarcely allows one to draw a breath, the exhilaration being further heightened by Carlos's precision articulation of every individual recorded note, which lends the music a machine-like quality that could only have been the outcome of electronic mediation. Envisaged in the context of the film, the music also gains an additional, hitherto unimagined and comically suggestive connotation as the backdrop to the notorious ménage-à-trois scene (the frame rate of which is itself dramatically sped up by Kubrick).

'Country Lane' (4:43) (Carlos/Elkind)
Another track that was conceived for the film (to accompany the scene in which the two policemen attempt to drown Alex) but was ultimately not used, 'Country Lane' is the second of the two original pieces that appear on the Columbia album and one that provides further fascinating insight into Carlos's emerging composer personality. Close listening will reveal that the main theme employed here is the aforementioned 'Dies Irae' chant, which is rhythmically re-worked, appearing by turns as a central melody, a low bass, and at one point, even as a vocoded sung element, often with a punctuating off-beat chordal accompaniment that adds to the overall strangeness.

For Carlos, the 'Dies Irae' tune, whose Latin setting (as part of the Requiem Mass) refers to the last judgment 'day of wrath', obviously has a symbolic relationship with the character of Alex, and by implication, the nature of evil more generally. It was not until her score for *The Shining* (1980), however, that she was able to employ the idea more forthrightly as a central theme (used to great effect in the film's dramatic opening tracking shot). Also of interest is the final section of 'Country Lane' (from 3:38), where we have the introduction of natural 'found sound' material – thunderstorms and rain – which (somewhat logically) gives way to a short vocoder-processed fragment of the melody of 'Singin' In The Rain', a tune inextricably associated with the home invasion sequence earlier in the film. With the appearance of this environmental evocation, the scene is very much set for the new world of sound explored by Carlos in *Sonic Seasonings*.

Sonic Seasonings (1972)

Personnel:
Wendy Carlos: Moog synthesizer, recording, composition and performance
Rachel Elkind: producer, vocals on 'Winter'
Record label: Columbia Records PG 31234
Format: Double LP
Recorded at Elkind 'Brownstone' Studio, West 87th St, Manhattan
Release date: 1972
Highest chart position: US: 2 (*Billboard* Classical LPs), 168 (*Billboard* 200)
Running time: 85:07

In the previously mentioned 1979 interview with Dominic Milano for
Contemporary Keyboard magazine, Carlos explained that *Sonic Seasonings*
had emerged during a period of downtime, which had caused a re-evaluation
of the musical direction she and Elkind had been exploring:

> We were having a little problem with Columbia, and they appeared to be
> disinterested in us because of not having a real artist that they could have
> in pictures and stuff and running around concertising, which is, after all,
> the way most record careers are carried through. Very few people just put
> things down on record. So, there was just not as much excitement as there
> had been in the beginning. And I just nastily said to Rachel, 'Well, if it's not
> gonna sell, and it's not gonna be available, then it doesn't matter what we
> do. Let's just do any old thing and put it on tape and release it.' It was really
> a mad gesture from a mind that's in a frenzy, just lashing out with things that
> don't really make sense. And we started out with, 'How about something
> to do with the four seasons? There are four of them, so we can make two
> records, one season per side, and we can use a lot of natural sounds. Let's
> see what we can do with it.'

From the public's perspective, *Sonic Seasonings* would also no doubt have
appeared as a rather unexpected development in Carlos's musical style. Her
profile thus far had been founded on a reputation for slickly produced and
virtuosically performed synthetic re-imaginings of iconic classical pieces, not
monolithic, abstract, experimental soundscapes that demanded a focused
listening approach. However, it is important to remember that *Switched-On
Bach* had been conceived as an experiment, not a defining musical statement,
whose fortuitous timing had enabled it to penetrate the imagination of a
public prepared to hear classical music in a different way. The fact was that
Carlos's musical development had been moving in the direction of a conception
like *Sonic Seasonings* for several years and, in particular, reflected her long
apprenticeship in the field of experimental electronic music. For example, in its
use of 'found' material (that is, the use of sounds recorded from the everyday
environment), the LP has an affinity with the *musique concrete* innovations

pioneered in Europe by composers such as Pierre Schaffer and Pierre Henry in the 1940s and 1950s, although as Carlos notes, she differs from these figures in that she does not tend to overly modify or process the sounds she employs, rather it is a question of the organisation of these unique sonic events within a time frame. In this sense, her work is closer to pieces such as Luc Ferrari's 'Presque Rien No. 1' (1967), which compresses a day's worth of seaside recordings into a concentrated listening experience.

Carlos's penchant for constructing new timbres from scratch can also be related to the work of Karlheinz Stockhausen in Cologne and Louis and Bebe Barron (composers of the iconic electronic music soundtrack for *Forbidden Planet*) in the United States. This combination of the pre-recorded sonic object with synthetically conceived material produces a potent mix, placing the album in the category of what is commonly known as 'electro-acoustic' music. Looking forward, certain aspects of *Sonic Seasonings* (on the track 'Winter', for example) also anticipate the emergence of a musical style that was to be later termed by Brian Eno as 'ambient', describing a minimalistic, slowly evolving and often repetitive conception that was designed to be 'as ignorable as it is interesting' (see Eno's classic 1975 *Discreet Music* album, for example). Indeed, Elkind's brief liner note states that 'these records were designed to be a part of the decor, so to speak – a sonic ambience that enhances the listener's total environment'. At times, the intensely machine-like aspects of the music, as heard on the track 'Summer', even ally the album with the 'noise' aesthetics of 1970s industrial music.

Seen from another angle, the fact that the music of *Sonic Seasonings* is purposefully conceived to describe real-world phenomena and convey a narrative – in this case, four vignettes designed to evoke feelings and ideas associated with the seasons – also links it to a long-established historical tradition of 'programmatic' music in the classical field. This includes (most famously) Vivaldi's *The Four Seasons* (c. 1720), Haydn's choral work *The Seasons* (1801), Glazunov's ballet *The Seasons* (1899) and numerous other pieces concerned with the evocation of nature, such as Beethoven's 'Pastoral' Symphony No. 6 (1808) and Delius's *On Hearing The First Cuckoo In Spring* (1912). Related to this are connections with musical Impressionism as espoused by the French composer Claude Debussy (1862-1918), including his three-movement orchestral work *La Mer* (1905), whose focus is on the sea and its ever-changing character. It is interesting to note that the cover of the sheet music edition of Debussy's score famously used the image of 'The Great Wave Off Kanagawa' by the Japanese artist Hokusai, which is echoed in the album artwork chosen by Carlos for *Sonic Seasonings*. The image in her case is taken from a large six-panel painting entitled 'Waves (or alternatively 'Islands') At Matsushima' by Japanese Edo artist Ogata Kôrin (1658-1716), which adorns the back and front covers of the gatefold sleeve. Kôrin's painting, which contains a dramatic depiction of a tempestuous sea that threatens to engulf three small rocky islands, has relevance to the sound images created by

Carlos on side three for 'Autumn', with its primary focus on water. The use of artwork in this manner is a significant development in the presentation and packaging of Carlos's music, the associated imagery now possessing a more serious purpose as a visual support to a musical concept. It is also a strategy that links the album closely to comparable trends in progressive rock at this time. It is worth noting that *Sonic Seasonings* was an important influence on Yes, specifically the album *Close To The Edge* (1972), whose beginning emulates Carlos's LP with its sounds of birds and flowing water.

A final important aspect of the presentation of *Sonic Seasonings*, which again relates the LP to 19th-century music, is its accompanying texts, including poems by Lord Byron, Emily Dickinson, the early Chinese poets Chu Shu Chen (c. 1200), Wang Wei (699-759) and P'Ei Ti (b. 714) and a biblical quotation from the 'Song Of Solomon'. Carlos also quotes a poem by her composer-performer student friend Philip Ramey (b. 1939), whose subject is the sun, here characterised as a somewhat oppressive force that drains life, which may have provided the inspiration for her uncompromising sonic setting of 'Summer'. While this and the other poems are obviously intended to be read while listening to the music, perhaps encouraging one to attach a narrative to the sonic experience, there is, however, no attempt to make an explicit link between poems and tracks. Also of interest is Ramey's extended biographical sleeve note for the LP, which recounts his friendship with Carlos since their initial meeting at Columbia University in 1962. There are insights here into Carlos's classical musical inclinations and her earlier electronic music compositions resulting from her time as a student at the Columbia-Princeton Electronic Music Center, some of which Ramey was involved in performing. While Ramey's sleeve note does not deal directly with *Sonic Seasonings* itself, other than to imply the work is a culminating point of her electronic music activities since *Switched-On Bach*, it nonetheless provides a musical context for the album's experiments. It is left to Elkind's shorter programme note to capture the essence of the LP, which she describes as an 'aural tapestry ... created from impressionistic and expressionistic experiences of nature' and an 'amalgam of the natural and synthetic'. Elkind also mentions that the natural sounds were recorded 'as realistically as possible' in Quad, a short-lived, early, four-speaker surround sound format which had been the LP's intended listening environment.

'Spring' (22:09)

In the opening track, Carlos paints an enthralling sonic portrait of the gradual awakening of nature, its central motif an ornithological one, expressed in a depiction of the dawn chorus. Heard either on good speakers or headphones, it is a deeply immersive listening experience, the serene and slowly unfolding music producing an attitude of calm contemplation.

0:00: The piece opens with the recorded sounds of birds chirruping, which Carlos has organised to suggest a certain rhythmic regularity. A few moments later, a high-pitched melodic line is heard. With its pipe-like timbre and improvised ornamental arabesques, this line is clearly intended to be suggestive of birdsong. The latter is also accompanied by sustained 'glassy' synthesizer harmonies, which outline a slowly evolving chord progression. This functions more as a backdrop, colouring the scene in the manner of the landscape in a painting rather than directing the music towards any particular harmonic goal.

6:39: A thunderclap marks the move into a new sonic environment. The recorded chirruping sounds continue, but the pipe-like sound has now been replaced with (Moog) synthesized melodic elements, including a 'twangy' sound whose repetitive phrases suggest a folk stringed instrument of some kind (a banjo perhaps?) and a comical plodding bass with an out of time feel. Following this, there is an extended section in which only the thunderstorm and the sounds of rain are heard and this gradually becomes more intense. At 10:08, rather unexpectedly, the sound of a jet plane is heard for a few moments, perhaps as a reminder that in the modern era, man-made machines are as much a part of 'nature' as organic entities. The thunderstorm continues, at 12:20 becoming combined once again with the repetitive, twangy, melodic idea and bass line. The twangy melody is heard in different octaves and in different tone colours.

14:22: Against the continuing storm, we once again begin to hear the sounds that opened the track, namely the high-pitched improvisatory birdsong-like melody and the glassy sustained synthesizer chords, which are, after a while, combined with the chirruping sounds we heard at the outset as the storm gradually clears. By 19:00, the long-note chords have dropped out and we are finally left with the melody and bird sounds alone. The high melody is then gradually dissipated and fragmented until only sporadic bird chirrups (treated to delay effects) remain.

'Summer' (21:31)

In pictorial terms, Carlos's musical response to the idea of summer captures something of the sounds of this season with its obvious nature effects – specifically, croaking frogs and buzzing insects – while the throbbing, pulsating electronic noises that permeate the piece conjure up a shimmering, almost oppressive heat. At the same time, our saturation in the sounds of sci-fi, since the unveiling of Louis and Bebe Barron's 'electronic tonalities' for the 1956 film *Forbidden Planet*, makes it just as easy for us to place ourselves in an alien landscape of strangely constituted and constantly mutating organic matter. Whichever way one prefers to imagine it, 'Summer' is unquestionably a dramatic and gripping listening experience from start to finish. In February 1973, *Gramophone*'s critic, William Somerville Mann, described 'Summer' as the 'most extreme movement' on the LP, which, in the generally positive terms of his review, implied the musical boundaries being pushed here by Carlos. For some critics, however, such as *Stereo Review*'s P.K in September

1972, the piece's apparent juxtaposition of the organic with machine-like was too much to bear:

> 'Summer' turned out to be as insufferable as the real thing, with what innocently started out sounding like a lawnmower but increased intolerably to the proportions of a giant buzz-saw, while the crickets and katydids sound effects were magnified beyond all toleration, as in some ghastly science-fiction epic.

In certain respects, 'Summer' even comes close to the ethos of early industrial music (of the Throbbing Gristle variety) in its use of gradually intensifying sounds that hypnotise and gradually overwhelm the listener, almost to the point of discomfort. In its accomplished sound design, it is obvious that Carlos has learned much from her work in the field of experimental electronic music, including the ability (very necessary when dealing with abstract materials) to craft an effective sonic narrative which holds the listener's attention throughout. From the perspective of the mix, this includes experimentation with the stereo field, including some dynamic movement of the sounds between the speakers later in the piece, which produces a disconcerting but, nonetheless, compelling effect. Somerville Mann even goes as far as suggesting that Carlos's piece is 'melodious', although not in the conventional sense, but as 'tone colour melody'.

'Fall' (20:56)

With 'Fall', which moves the focus of the seasonal narrative to the coastline, we are treated to some of the LP's most ravishing environmental sounds, water being a particularly prominent ingredient of the sonic landscape. In comparison to the first two movements, there is also much conventionally conceived musical material performed on the synthesizer, with clearly identifiable, attractively designed melodies and a feeling of harmonic progression with key shifts which move the music forward.

'Fall' opens with soothing sounds of rushing water, effectively dousing the flames of the preceding movement. High brass-like sounds enter shortly after in a beautiful brass-like chorale-like passage, which, at first, appears obscured by the waves before becoming more prominent. A little while later, we begin to hear occasional cries of seagulls overhead. From 3:50, the piece begins to develop more rhythmic momentum with the introduction of a repeating figure, which accompanies a melody on a horn-like instrument.

At 6:20, we move into a rather different environmental setting, signalling a structural change. The flowing water is still present but now recedes into the background, our attention shifting at this point to the sound of a piercing wind and then the crackling of a fire. Wisps of a free-form, flute-like melody are heard distantly. During this segment, the listener seems situated (using spatial effects) in an interior space somewhat removed from the elements, taking shelter.

At 8.25, fragments of a new musical idea, repetitive in character, are introduced, which coalesce to form an accompaniment to a folk-like melody, together with occasional interjections by the flute-like instrument. From 9:37, the texture begins to thicken gradually in the lower end. At the same time, we hear the gentle sounds of cattle lowing in the background, which act as a kind of pad.

From 11:10, the fire returns with an increased intensity and Carlos employs a spatial effect to create a sense of a larger, more cavernous space. This gives way to low, brassy sounds, which begin to build in a gradually thickening texture, the flute once again interjecting at intervals.

After 13:00, we begin to hear the sounds of water and seagulls once again, suggesting a return to the environment from which the music had originally emerged (in other words, a recapitulation of the first section). At 15:11, we welcome the re-entry of the chorale-like material and the repose it brings, eventually giving way to the beautiful accompanied horn melody heard earlier, which now concludes the piece.

'Winter' (20:31)

For the LP's finale, Carlos convincingly evokes, through the medium of sound, a world of ice and snow, whose sole inhabitants are a group of wolves that call to each other across the windswept terrain. In its evocation of stasis and timelessness, 'Winter' arguably comes closest of the four tracks to the idea of ambient music. It is a music of pure atmosphere, whose gradually morphing sounds provide the perfect sonic analogue to a frozen landscape shaded by a subtly changing light. The movement begins with crystalline piano-like timbres and the sounds of shaken metallic percussion, followed by long sustained tones on the synthesizer, which combine to produce bare-sounding chord structures. These elements are then joined by a white noise generated (or possibly recorded) howling wind, which permeates the musical sound world. A significant portion of the track is devoted to the maintenance of this relatively unchanging – but, at the same time, subtly evolving – sonic landscape, and then from around 8:30, there is a gradual increase in intensity until we begin to hear the sporadic howls of wolves at 10:10. Although one is certainly anticipating something of interest to emerge from the drone-laden texture, whose immutable nature naturally engenders a sense of expectation, this is a remarkable and surprising direction for the piece to take. After a while, the wolves recede into the distance but then suddenly re-merge into the foreground at 14:03, now heard over a low bass note on the Moog. This sudden grounding of the music in the lower end of the frequency spectrum contrasts dramatically with the generally higher-pitched emphasis of the soundscape thus far and serves to mark the inception of the final section of the piece. From this point onwards, the wolves' howling builds up into a multi-layered and delay-effected collage, ultimately crowned by Elkind's improvised vocals, which match the patterning of the howls, until she is finally left singing alone over an ominous passage of deep-toned chords performed on Moog.

Switched-On Bach II (1973)

Personnel:
Wendy Carlos: Moog synthesizer, Yamaha Electone E-5, performance, arranging, recording and production
Rachel Elkind: producer
Record label: Columbia Records S 65974
Format: LP
Recorded at Elkind 'Brownstone' Studio, West 87th St, Manhattan
Release date: Late 1973
Highest chart position: US: 5 (*Billboard* Classical LPs)
Running time: 39:10

Previously, it was pointed out that, on account of the innovations in recording and arranging observed on *The Well-Tempered Synthesizer*, the latter could hardly be regarded as merely a follow-up cash-in on *Switched-On Bach*'s success. With *Switched-On Bach II*, however, such an accusation is more difficult to refute. Already, the title puts one in mind of the predictably lacklustre movie sequel, while the album art, representing Bach as an astronaut floating in space – umbilically attached to a synthesizer module – places the recording in the territory of the frivolous that Carlos had reacted against with *Switched-On Bach*. In addition, there is something of a re-tread of the Bach programming formula here, with side one of the LP once again focused on popular miniatures by the composer, all of which would have been very familiar to classical music audiences, including 'Sheep May Safely Graze' and the Badinerie from the Suite No. 2 in B minor. Side two's more substantial and ambitiously rendered item is once again a Brandenburg Concerto, this time No. 5.

Furthermore, it is notable that, unlike *Switched-On Bach* and *The Well-Tempered Synthesizer*, the sleeve notes provided with *Switched-On Bach II*'s original LP release give no information whatsoever about how the album was made or even provide concert programme-style commentary on the individual musical excerpts. Instead, we have a personal account by Robert Moog (certainly valuable in its own terms) of his evolving working relationship with Carlos since 1965, which sheds more light on the background of *Switched-On Bach* than its more recent successor. Omitting to focus on either the music or the technological wizardry harnessed in its realisation ultimately tends to downplay the listening experience, which is unfortunate given that the album, despite its reliance upon previously well-honed sounds and production tricks, represents a considerable achievement where the evolution of Carlos's synthesizer-based aesthetic is concerned.

Thankfully, with the later (1999) ESD re-release (81622), which includes a more extended sleeve note, Carlos has provided some useful information about the making of *Switched-On Bach II*. Firstly, she points out that the album was created in response to repeated requests from fans via CBS to create further synthesizer arrangements of Bach. The implication here is that she was now in an appropriate frame of mind to consider producing another album of music in a genre that she had already explored extensively, having devoted time to developing original music concepts for *A Clockwork Orange* and *Sonic Seasonings*. An important technological factor also contributed to Carlos's enthusiasm for revisiting Bach, namely her acquisition of the recently released (1971) Yamaha Electone E-5 electronic organ. This was a polyphonic instrument and, thus, an advance on the Moog's single-line limitations, allowing for the performance of chords and complex contrapuntal lines while, at the same time, adding new colouristic potential to her sonic armoury. In particular, the Electone was employed by Carlos to facilitate the recording of the complicated harpsichord part in the Brandenburg Concerto No. 5.

On its release in late 1973, *Switched-On Bach II* was eagerly consumed by audiences, selling (according to a *Cashbox* magazine report) 50,000 copies in the first week. Its success was a considerable achievement given that Carlos's formula for electronically re-thinking classical music had now been out in the open for five years and readily available for imitation by competitors. Pretenders to the Carlos throne included, for example, Hans Wurman, whose 1970 releases *The Moog Strikes Bach* and *Chopin À La Moog* attempted to up the game by broadening the range of classical material beyond Baroque era music (Mozart, Chopin, Rachmaninov and Prokofiev). Recordings featuring the Moog in performances of jazz and popular music, alongside quirkily re-worked classical pieces, had also begun to saturate the marketplace, including the efforts of Gershon Kingsley (the author of the quintessential Moog classic 'Popcorn') and Jean-Jacques Perrey, which were widely influential. It was thus clear that, relative to these developments, Carlos had retained her fanbase, who showed no signs of tiring of what she had to offer in this area.

Switched-On Bach II also received a generally positive reception from the critical establishment, including further approval from the UK's premier classical recordings periodical *Gramophone*, whose reviewer Edward Greenfield wrote in June 1974, using Carlos's birth identity, that 'even by the standards of computer interpretations of Bach, this is very good indeed – compulsive listening. Plainly, Carlos is in a class of his own. I predict great success once again.' It is interesting that Greenfield should have assumed the involvement of a computer in Carlos's recording process, which reflected a misconception, widespread amongst non-technical types, that such machines were at this time capable of generating complex multi-part musical performances. As it was, Carlos did not use a computer to synthesize Bach until 1992, on the album *Switched-On Bach 2000*.

'Selections From Suite No. 2 In B minor', BWV 1067
Switched-On Bach II begins with three selections from Bach's famous Orchestral Suite No. 2 In B minor, composed around 1738. In its original

form, this Suite comprises seven movements in total; thus, Carlos appears to have been discerning in her choices, which were presumably influenced by their suitability for a Moog treatment. The music was originally scored for a four-part string ensemble and is notable for featuring the 'transverse' flute as a prominent solo (or *concertante*) instrument, which comes to the fore particularly strongly in the Badinerie. As expected, Carlos's synthesizer realisations exceed the limitations presented by Bach's, for the most part, monochrome instrumentation, portraying familiar music in a vibrant new light.

Badinerie (1:25)
A *badinerie* (a French word which means 'jesting') is a fast piece in 2/4 time, which usually begins with an upbeat. Such movements are also typically in binary form – that is, in two sections, each of which is repeated once – as is the case here. Instrumentally, the piece shows off the agility of the flute to great effect, which, in Bach's original score, is the top-line focal point throughout. Given that maintaining a single-tone colour for the flute part would likely pall in this synthetic context, Carlos's approach instead is to vary the timbres used on each repeat, some of which are flute-like in character, others rather less so.

Minuet (1:20)
Carlos's rendering of this charming Minuet (a dance in three beats to the bar) at times borders on the schmaltzy, largely as a result of the vibrato employed on the held notes. In addition to the subtly varying tone colours, the listener will also observe that Carlos is once again employing the hocketing effect here – that is, the breaking up of the phrases across instrumental parts, highlighted by left/right stereo positioning – developed in her previous realisations of the Scarlatti Sonatas. The approach in this case was perhaps influenced by the fact that in Bach's original score, the flute line simply doubles the first violin part, which would not have been very interesting to emulate on the synthesizer.

Bourrée (1:40)
The selection concludes with an up-tempo Bourrée (to be precise, this is actually Bourrée I and Bourrée II of Bach's Suite combined), a French-originated dance form we have already encountered on *The Well-Tempered Synthesizer* (in the Handel Suite). As is typical, each Bourrée is in binary form, with each section played twice before a final 'Da Capo' (meaning go back to the beginning) – in other words, we have a final run through the first Bourrée in its entirety, but this time, without repeating the sections. A notable feature of the first Bourrée is its four-note ostinato (i.e. looped) pattern in the bass, while the second is more sparsely textured with a call-and-answer type interaction between the busy top line flute, the inner parts

and the bass. It will be noticed in the latter that Carlos adopts the same approach to colouristic variation of the flute part in the repeats as she did in the Badinerie.

Two-Part Invention In A Minor, BWV 784 (1:20)

Bach's Two-Part Inventions, some of which (No. 4, 8 and 14) we have already encountered on the first *Switched-On Bach* LP, are among the composer's most economically conceived contrapuntal pieces, in which the weight of the music is concentrated in two carefully constructed lines. Like Carlos's first efforts, in the Invention In A Minor (No. 13), we find that stereo placement of the individual parts is once again an important strategy in clarifying the individual musical elements, here married with the now-familiar hocketing technique to fragment the line further. The result is a more complex texture, amplifying Bach's sparsely conceived broken chord interchange between treble and bass.

Two-Part Invention In A Major, BWV 783 (1:10)

The Invention In A Major (No. 12) is an exciting piece, utilising the trill (a rapid decoration of a single note) as a distinctive feature, which is heard alternately in the high and low registers. As in the Invention In A Minor, we can hear that the fast-running passages have been fragmented to give the impression of a greater number of parts, and we even have the displacement of individual notes into different octaves to generate additional counter-melodies. While this might amount to something of a distortion of the original material (at least from the perspective of an authentic Bach keyboard performance), the effect is to generate a greater range of colours. As ever, the music is rendered by Carlos with exacting precision, resulting in an exhilarating listening experience.

'Sheep May Safely Graze' From Cantata No. 208 (5:00)

Another perennial Bach favourite, 'Sheep May Safely Graze' is an aria for a soprano voice taken from the so-called 'Hunt' Cantata No. 208. Like the previously discussed 'Air On A G String', the piece has appeared in numerous instrumental arrangements, which have helped to make it a popular standard. The translated text of the original aria is:

Sheep may safely graze where a good shepherd is watching.
Where a ruler governs well one may look for peace, freedom, and a happy people.

The original music consists of a sparse texture of two recorder parts (referred to as flutes in Bach's time), the soprano voice and a bass line (sometimes described as a continuo part, usually fleshed out with keyboard chords). As a piece that reflects the more lyrical side of Bach, being heavily reliant upon a lead melody line supported by a steadily pulsing accompaniment, there is little of the composer's interactive partwriting to inspire Carlos in developing a colourful synthesizer treatment. Instead, we have a fairly uniform setting (the Electone's contribution is quite apparent here) comprising two main contrasting timbres – one treated with somewhat excessive vibrato for the through-composed soprano melody and a pipe-like sound for the recurrent double flute commentary – which persist throughout. There are also piano-like punctuating chords filling out the harmony and a sustained bass timbre that becomes a little overpowering. It is, nonetheless, expressively performed music, even if the arrangement borders on the treacly.

Suite From Anna Magdelena Notebook
Anna Magdelena (1701-1760) was Bach's second wife, who, in addition to bearing the composer 13 children and running his domestic affairs, also found time to act as a copyist for his music. Here, Carlos has created a Suite of four pieces taken from the second *Notenbüchlein Für Anna Magdalena Bach* of 1725. This is a collection of music which comprises a number of compositions by Bach but also several pieces by contemporaries admired by the composer and his wife (hence the prefix 'Anh' rather than 'BWV' in the Bach catalogue, which means 'doubtful attribution').

Musette In D Major, Anh. 126 (mistakenly numbered as 216 on the album sleeve) (1:10)
This piece (whose authorship by Bach is confirmed) is written in the style of the musette, a dance-like piece evocative of folk music and characterised by simple, clear, repeating melodic phrases and a drone bass which emulates the bagpipe. Carlos appears to have gone for something of a comedic effect in her synthesizer realisation (observe, in particular, the offbeat quasi-vocal 'ahh' interjections in the first section).

Minuet In G Major, Anh. 114 (1:40)
This charming and very well-known Minuet (often appearing in beginner books for piano and other instruments) is not by Bach. It is taken from a Suite for Harpsichord by Christian Petzold (1677-1733). Carlos keeps this simple piece interesting with a range of what are, by now, trademark synthesizer colours, which help to draw out the characterful, melodic parts (the stereo picture is also harnessed to good effect).

'Bist Du Bei Mir', BWV 508 (2:15)
Another piece mistakenly attributed to Bach, this beautiful hymn-like melody, meaning 'If you are with me', has been shown in recent years to have been written by his contemporary, the composer Gottfried Heinrich Stölzel (1690-1749). In the notebook, the melody is quite sparsely arranged in two parts, whereas Carlos's synthesizer version has a fully developed harmonic

accompaniment, which is presented in a brass/wind-like orchestration. My assumption here is that this is a new realisation that has been undertaken by Carlos specially for the recording.

Marche In D Major, Anh. 122 (1:00)

The Marche, whose authorship is commonly attributed to Bach's son Carl Philipp Emmanuel Bach (1714-1788), is a sprightly number clothed in a mixture of brassy and sparkling bell-like synthesizer timbres, punctuated with emulated cymbal sounds.

Brandenburg Concerto No. 5 In D Major, BWV 1050
Allegro (10:45)

The Allegro is a substantial movement, and, in fact, it is the longest to be found in all the Brandenburg Concertos. Its increased length is primarily due to the focus Bach places on the harpsichord, which is now given a central soloistic role – in other words, it is here doing much more than just providing the underlying chordal accompaniment to the other instruments. Like the third and fourth Brandenburg Concertos previously discussed, this movement employs the *ritornello* form, featuring a section of music with a strongly identifiable melody, which is heard at the beginning of the piece performed by the whole ensemble and returns periodically in different keys. In between are contrasting sections (called 'episodes'), allowing for more focus on individual solo instruments (flute and violin), which often interact with one another in a call-and-response type manner. The harpsichord (whose metallic sound Carlos has carefully emulated) has its first notable solo entry at 2:10, a short section featuring a series of fast runs, which are segmented between the two speakers in a manner we are now quite accustomed to. Also of note is the wonderful section that begins at 3:50, in which the harpsichord accompanies, via clockwork-like repeating arpeggios, a series of broken chord bass figures which move gradually downwards, becoming progressively quieter. More fireworks appear at 6:30 following the penultimate *ritornello*, which gives way to another section of fast harpsichord scales and arpeggios, leading into the cadenza section at 7:12. At this point, all the other instruments drop out, leaving the focus entirely on the keyboard soloist – Carlos. In this extended section, a range of tone colours are employed to bring the different voices of the harpsichord part to life, the sounds being distributed across the stereo field to produce a larger-than-life sound more suggestive of a harpsichord ensemble than one instrument alone. The culmination of this section prior to the entry of the final *ritornello* is breathtaking.

Affetuoso (5:35)

The slow movement which follows – now scored for a reduced ensemble comprising only the two solo instruments and the harpsichord continuo (playing a bass line with chords) – contains some very intricate part writing with much imitation. In contrast to the effusive first movement, the piece is also in a minor key, possessing a mournful character as if the composer is labouring a heavy sorrow. One thing that is quite noticeable is the tendency of a different instrument to lead each recurrence of the main tune (which has a characteristic swung feel), beginning with the violin, then followed by the flute, and eventually the harpsichord. In fact, this music also employs a subtle *ritornello* form, which can be appreciated in the contrasts between the ensemble statements of the tune and the solo passages in which certain instruments are exposed. Carlos's synthesizer conception is a straightforward one, maintaining the impression of a small ensemble comprising instruments whose timbres resemble their real-world counterparts.

Allegro (4:50)

Like the Brandenburg Concerto No. 4, this movement, which now sees the return of the full ensemble, blends the *ritornello* idea with the fugue structure. This is immediately apparent from the outset as the dance-like theme is imitated through a series of entries in different voices across the ensemble, eventually culminating in a stretto (a point at which the entries occur very quickly, one after the other). The harpsichord is once again a dominant solo force in this movement, taking the limelight in the captivating section, which begins with a series of impudent trills at 2:22, while the ensemble later rejoins to interject punctuating comments. Carlos's hocketing technique is used with great skill to dramatise the music from here to the end of the movement, enhanced by dynamic stereo shifting, as well as the manipulation of depth proximity to make some sounds appear 'in your face' and others in a rather more resonant setting. Once again, we are reminded that this is very much a studio-conceived interpretation of Bach that could not have existed in the concert hall.

By Request (1975)

Personnel:
Wendy Carlos: Moog synthesizer, composition, performance and arranging
Rachel Elkind: producer
Philip Ramey: piano on 'Dialogues For Piano And Two Loudspeakers' and 'Episodes For Piano And Electronic Sound'
Record label: Columbia Masterworks M 32088/CBS 73163
Format: LP
Recorded at Elkind 'Brownstone' Studio, West 87th St, Manhattan
Release date: November 1975
Highest chart position: US: 6 (*Billboard* Classical LPs)
Running time: 45:32

By Request is a miscellany album whose content was, to a certain extent, determined by Carlos's fans' suggestions for new pieces to add to her electronic repertory, although, as it turned out, prototypes of a number of the tracks had sometimes been completed several years earlier. A short press release in *Billboard* on 8 November 1975 outlined the process by which the album's repertoire had been selected:

> The concept of the album was the result of a postcard survey undertaken in 1972-73. The cards were included in Carlos's *Sonic Seasonings* album and invited buyers to suggest repertoire to be used in a new album. More than 5,000 replies were received, according to Rachel Elkind, Carlos's producer.

The LP sees Carlos expanding beyond the classical music remit to encompass a broader range of material, including electronic re-imaginings of two pop songs – The Beatles' 'Eleanor Rigby' and Burt Bacharach and Hal David's 'What's New Pussycat?' – as well as three original compositions, two of which – the 'Dialogues For Piano And Two Loudspeakers' and 'Episodes For Piano And Electronic Sound' – are of an experimental nature. With the exception of Bach, who appears twice on the LP, the classical selections are drawn from 19th and early 20th-century music (Tchaikovsky, Wagner and Elgar) and would have been widely familiar to concert-going audiences. At face value, in its eclectic compilation of musical styles, the LP does not thus far appear to be particularly innovative for 1975, where the synthesizer genre is concerned. More than five years had now passed since *Switched-On Bach*, in which time a large number of Moog-focused recordings had reached the marketplace, pushing the fad for electronic re-workings of popular and other forms of music to saturation point. At the same time, the Moog synthesizer and comparable instruments by newcomers, such as ARP (the 2600) and EMS (the VCS3), had begun to proliferate widely in popular music, becoming a mainstay of progressive rock (ELP, Pink Floyd, Genesis, Rick Wakeman), as well as appearing in commercial pop (Hot Butter, Chicory Tip). In addition,

German groups emerging from the Krautrock scene, such as Kraftwerk and Tangerine Dream, had begun to carve out a new musical aesthetic unique to the synthesizer, which had little to do with referencing past music genres. While such developments indicated that the synthesizer arrangements of existing music were certainly becoming passé, this is by no means to denigrate Carlos's efforts in this recording, which continues to display the technical accomplishment and distinctiveness of style that fans had come to expect.

On closer examination, the programming of the LP is also not as orthodox as one might imagine. The inclusion of the two experimental electronic pieces, for example, appears as a bold step when heard in relation to the more traditional selections (arriving straight after Tchaikovsky on side one), suggesting an unwillingness to compromise on Carlos's part. Moreover, the arrangements of more hackneyed pieces on the album, such as Wagner's 'Wedding March', do not always resort to conventional readings of the music. Carlos's continued commitment to Bach also yields another fascinating account of a Brandenburg Concerto, the First Movement of No. 2 in this instance, while the most accessible original piece, 'Geodesic Dance', affords an enjoyable stereophonic listening experience. Finally, the substantial concluding track (and undoubted highlight of the LP) is an ingenious potpourri of well-known melodies drawn from a range of classical and popular pieces, skilfully worked around one of Elgar's most iconic tunes, reminding us that Carlos is also an imaginatively playful composer. Ultimately, this combination of perspectives makes it difficult to dismiss the LP as a mere trifling, light music compilation. It is also worth noting that from the perspective of the LP's packaging, we have a return to the format of the early Carlos albums with the inclusion of sleeve notes by *Switched-On Bach/The Well-Tempered Synthesizer* collaborator Benjamin Folkman, which reinstate the previous pattern of providing programme note-style commentary on each album track. The observations which follow should be regarded as a supplement to these.

Three Dances From 'Nutcracker Suite' (5:24) (Pyotr Ilyich Tchaikovsky)

Pyotr Ilyich Tchaikovsky (1840-1893) remains one of the most popular classical composers of the late 19th century; his highly melodic sensibilities and imaginative orchestration appear well suited to the predominantly popular ethos of *By Request*. Here, Carlos has opted to cover three movements from his most famous ballet suite The Nutcracker, Op. 71a, which dates from 1892. These are extremely well-known pieces, the fantastical subject matter of which elicits an effective synthesizer treatment from Carlos in which she captures the essence of Tchaikovsky's original instrumentation without necessarily aiming to faithfully copy it. The arrangements are, on the whole, well-executed performances (as with *Switched-On Bach*, painstakingly pieced together from multiple individual takes) and serve to usher us once again into the familiar

Carlos sound world. Folkman, in fact, found their effect so convincingly musical that, for him, they represented 'the state of the electronic art'.

A. 'Russian Dance'
Known commonly as the Trepak (a Russian/Ukrainian folk dance), Carlos manages to render this famous music with an energy that matches the more familiar orchestral performances. There is something of the atmosphere of her *A Clockwork Orange* aesthetic in the sound of the arrangement, due no doubt in part to the frenetic speed at which it is performed, reminding us of her almost machine-like setting of the William Tell Overture.

B. 'Dance Of The Sugar-Plum Fairy'
One of the most famous of the composer's pieces, 'Dance Of The Sugar Plum Fairy' is distinguished by its atmospheric use of the celesta, an instrument that had been used by few composers until Tchaikovsky's time. Carlos produces a convincing synthesis of this sound here, as well as capturing the mysteriousness of the original score's low reed instruments (the bass clarinet especially). The middle section from 0:43-1:09, with its stabbing chords and arabesques bouncing between the left and right speakers, is highly effective.

C. 'Dance Of The Reed-Pipes'
The execution of this charming music (its original title is actually 'Dance Of The Mirlitons') is notable for Carlos's treatment of dynamic contrasts (in other words, gradations of soft/loud), with the music at times appearing to jump out of the speakers (see the middle section from 1:10-1:38). Appropriately for the subject matter of the piece, Carlos's synthesizer timbres possess a hollow and somewhat metallic character, which is at times reminiscent of the accordion.

Dialogues For Piano And Two Loudspeakers (4:00) (Carlos)
The Dialogues arrive with something of a shock after the Tchaikovsky, demanding a significant reorientation on the part of the listener. This piece and the Episodes For Piano And Electronic Sound, which come after it, date back to the days of Carlos's fledgling composing activities at the Columbia-Princeton Electronic Music Center in the mid-1960s, both being freshly re-recorded for the new LP. Carlos has described the piece (one of her earliest acknowledged compositions) as having a 'rhapsodic' character and tells us that there are two themes that are developed and transformed at some length, although these are not melodies in a traditional tonal sense (in other words, the music is not in a recognisable home key). The listener unaccustomed to the music's challenging abstract style might best approach this piece with the title firmly in mind, understanding that this is a conversation between the piano and electronic sounds. Focusing one's attention on the electronic element, whose repertoire of noises and spatial tricks is typical of the avant-garde electronic music idiom at this time, is a rewarding experience. The

piano soloist here and in the next piece is Philip Ramey, who successfully holds his own against the machine.

Episodes For Piano And Electronic Sound (5:50) (Carlos)

Folkman's sleeve notes for the LP release observe that this piece was created at the Columbia-Princeton Electronic Music Center and was realised (in other words, brought to life as a performance) in Carlos's basement studio at his parents' house in Providence, Rhode Island in the summer of 1964. The music, as the title suggests, is essentially episodic, in some ways behaving like a theme and variations, and relative to the Dialogues, is, on the whole, more accessible to the listener – Folkman describes it as 'expressive' and even 'romantic' in character. Certainly, the opening piano theme has a more traditional melodic shape that enables it to be readily identifiable on each recurrence, while some of the chordal passages, such as the solo piano segment at 0:23, are almost suggestive of jazz or conventional classical music. The piano's role varies throughout the piece, sometimes appearing solo, sometimes acting as an accompanist to the electronic element, and other times engaging in call and response. Compared to the Dialogues, the pianist's material is more challenging to perform, becoming increasingly virtuosic towards the end (from 3:33 onwards) as its interactions with the electronic element reach a crescendo. The electronic conception itself should not be seen as a throwaway gimmick – it is a carefully composed entity with a distinctive, somewhat humorous musical character of its own.

Geodesic Dance (3:21) (Carlos)

Regarding the title, Folkman's sleeve notes enlighten us by stating that Carlos had observed that 'certain ratios of the geodesic could be 'translated' into extremely subtle dance rhythms'. This is the sum total of information we have to go on, from which we can draw the general conclusion that mathematical principles underpin the structural thinking of this 'Electronic Etude'. Knowing the meaning of the word 'geodesic' does not necessarily assist in our appreciation of the music, of course, although one can certainly observe that there is a rigorous 'worked out' character to the material which is brought to life in stereophonically rendered three-dimensionality (Folkman comments that the piece was, in fact, originally an 'experiment in quadrophonic spatial locations'). Overall, Geodesic Dance is a quirky little number that holds the attention largely on account of its unpredictable form, which keeps the listener guessing as to where it will go next.

Brandenburg Concerto No. 2 In F Major, First Movement (5:50) (Johann Sebastian Bach)

According to Carlos's sleeve notes for the 2003 ESD re-release, this single Brandenburg Concerto movement is what remains of a first attempt at synthesizing all three movements, the second and third ultimately being shelved until the release of *Switched-On Brandenburgs* in 1980. The original scoring is for a mixed *concertino* (soloists group) consisting of a high 'clarino' trumpet (of the type famously heard in The Beatles' 'Penny Lane'), recorder, oboe and violin, which are accompanied by the usual *ripieno* string ensemble with keyboard continuo. Carlos's approach, as we have encountered repeatedly in her Brandenburg settings, is to approximate the sounds of these various instruments, as can be most clearly heard in the short solo sections in which they are individually exposed (e.g. the series of episodes between 0:35-1:04 and 2:52-3:14). However, in the latter part of the piece, it is clear that this authenticity has been abandoned for a more synthesizer-specific aesthetic, assisted by reverberant production values. As Folkman observes in his liner notes, the high trumpet part is surprisingly subdued in Carlos's rendition (to appreciate this, it is worth comparing this arrangement to traditional orchestral performances).

'Little' Fugue In G Minor (3:44) (Johann Sebastian Bach)
Carlos undertook her realisation of Bach's Fugue In G Minor (BWV 578) not long after she had completed *Switched-On Bach*. It is one of Bach's best-known fugues, sporting a memorable melodic subject (heard at the outset), which then appears in a variety of contrapuntal combinations. As observed earlier in this book, Carlos often achieved her best results when working with music of a linear nature, as it encouraged her to develop individually distinctive synthesizer timbres to delineate and distinguish the various parts. Her synthesizer treatment here retains something of the larger-than-life majesty of its organ sound, the presentation of the intricate musical detail being aided by studio production techniques (precise stereo positioning of the voices and subtle spatial effects).

'What's New Pussycat?' (2:05) (Burt Bacharach and Hal David)
'What's New Pussycat?' was written for the film of that name by the songwriting team of Burt Bacharach and Hal David in 1965. It is best known in the version performed by Tom Jones, for whom it was a hit single, and has since been covered by numerous other artists. According to Folkman's sleeve notes, Carlos's electronic version dates back to 1967 and is described as one of her first synthesizer pieces. It is interesting to note that, prior to appearing on *By Request,* it was released as a 45-rpm single in both the US (1972) and the UK (1973), appearing respectively as a B-side to The Beatles' 'Eleanor Rigby' (Columbia 4-45741) and as an A-side to Tchaikovsky's 'Dance Of The Reed Pipes' (S CBS 3590). Carlos's version successfully conjures up a circus-like/fairground atmosphere, featuring a prominent steam organ sound (perhaps inspired by the accordion in the original) and an 'oompah' bass. The track is laced with humour, its synthesizer imitations of cat meows being only one of a plethora of whacky electronic sounds that bombard the listener, anticipating the unorthodox treatment of the Second Movement

of Brandenburg's Concerto No. 3. Overall, 'What's New Pussycat?' evokes
the sense of adventure Carlos must have felt as she embarked on her early
synthesizer experiments.

'Eleanor Rigby' (2:06) (John Lennon and Paul McCartney)
As noted above, 'Eleanor Rigby' first appeared as a 45-rpm format single
in 1972, although Folkman's sleeve notes state that the arrangement was
actually completed as early as 1970. The choice to arrange a Beatles melody
is hardly surprising given the group's dominant cultural position during the
1960s and the standing of Lennon and McCartney, who were then counted
among the most important songwriters of the period, even being held in high
esteem within the cloistered classical music establishment. In this sense, one
can see why 'Eleanor Rigby', with its elaborate melody and dynamic string
arrangement, would have appealed to Carlos, as it is a piece that is, to some
extent, already in classical music territory ('Yesterday' might also have been
another suitable choice in these terms), giving her plenty of musical meat to
work with. While Carlos is faithful to the musical content of the original song
(including the stabbing string chords of the George Martin arrangement), her
electronic setting, enhanced by effects, considerably transforms its character.

Wedding March (Based On The Bridal Chorus From Lohengrin)
(1:12) (Richard Wagner)
This perennially popular wedding favourite by Richard Wagner (1813-1883)
is so ubiquitous in Western culture that its synthesizer treatment was going
to have to raise some eyebrows if it was not to pass unnoticed. Carlos's
very brief (and to the point) arrangement is clearly intended as a parody,
beginning with a full statement of the iconic melody in a chordal setting,
whose excessive vibrato elicits a mild seasickness. This is then followed by
a fast comical variation, which comprises a jazz-style walking bass under an
off-beat accompaniment, interrupted by arpeggio and scale flourishes that
ricochet around the stereo image. An unexpected pop song-like key change
at 1:01 signals the fragmentation and collapse of the piece into its final
chord.

**'Pompous Circumstances' (Variations & Fantasy On A Theme By
Elgar)** (12:00) (Carlos/Edward Elgar)
In his sleeve notes, Folkman describes 'Pompous Circumstances' as a
'miniaturised 17th-century German dance partita'; in other words, a collection
of pieces that use different dance forms (many examples of which we have
heard on previous albums). The piece is, in essence, a theme and variations
(with interludes) on the melody of 'Land Of Hope And Glory' by Edward
Elgar (1857-1934), in which Carlos explores a wide variety of musical styles
and references numerous famous pieces. Carlos's compositional dexterity is
on full display here, as she convincingly (and often amusingly) shoehorns the

Elgar tune into the musical structures of a number of well-known classics, including Ravel's 'Bolero' and 'Hail To The Chief'. Carlos's use of the Elgar melody also inevitably recalls her *A Clockwork Orange* soundtrack (Warner Bros release), where it appeared in its orchestral guise rather than as a synthesizer arrangement. Direct references to the latter are also found in her re-use of the William Tell Overture, which interjects at 3:55 as a brief accompaniment to the Elgar tune. However, Carlos is also paying homage to Elgar's famous orchestral work 'Enigma Variations', Folkman observing that each episode refers to 'friends and prominent personalities' (whose names are not revealed) and that it may be possible to 'discern political content'.

Another interesting aspect of 'Pompous Circumstances' relates to the issues surrounding its original UK release when the track was blocked via copyright law by the Elgar estate (Elgar's music was not public domain at this point). The full story can be found in the liner notes for the later ESD release of the album; suffice to say that the reasons related to a misunderstanding that Carlos was lampooning Elgar's sacred melody rather than, in her words, offering an 'affectionate new take'. This led to the track being replaced on UK releases by a compilation of pieces from the earlier *Well-Tempered Synthesizer* album. Carlos recalls that, on discovering this, she 'became silently livid, knowing that the record buying public and our many loyal fans in Britain, one of my favourite places, had been cheated'. This ban, incidentally, appears to have been extended to other releases within the European zone, too – the Netherlands edition (CBS 80028), for example, replaces 'Pompous Circumstances' with a shorter five-minute number entitled 'Stay Tuned', a compilation of radio jingles created in collaboration with Robert B. Schwartz. The following are some of the key musical events to look out for in the track.

0:00 – The introduction, which quotes from marching band composer John Philip Sousa's instantly recognisable 'Stars And Stripes Forever', followed by a full statement of Elgar's 'Land Of Hope And Glory' complete with percussion.

1:01 – A segue into the familiar 'Promenade' melody from Modest Mussorgsky's *Pictures At An Exhibition* (a piece that has famously been treated to several different re-workings, including a synthesiser version by Emerson, Lake and Palmer).

1:34 – At this point, we are in the territory of old-time American variety music, including references to Stephen Foster's 'Camptown Races' and ragtime music in the style of Scott Joplin.

2:33 – Now, we encounter a superlative synthesizer imitation of bagpipe music (referred to by Carlos as 'Piperpomp') performed by a marching band that appears to move across the stereo picture from left to right.

3:04 – A skilful conflation of Maurice Ravel's 'Bolero' with the Elgar tune.

3:56 – A synthetic timpani roll introduces the aforementioned William Tell Overture, which appears to fit nicely with the Elgar theme.

4:20 – A transitional section in which the theme is given a contrapuntal treatment in the manner of Bach.

4:57 – Rossini returns again, this time with a reference to an aria from the opera *The Barber Of Seville.*

5:21 – The next section appears to be a potpourri of variations on the Elgar melody reworked into various well-known tunes, beginning with a quotation in the style of the US Presidential anthem 'Hail To The Chief'. Also recognisable is a passage from the overture to Wagner's opera *Die Meistersinger* at 5:43.

6:22 – In this section, we are treated to a virtuosic collage of various melodic phrases from Elgar's Pomp and Circumstance marches.

7:58 – At the interlude, the music moves into a darkly atmospheric mood, putting one very much in mind of 'Timesteps', thus, once again, evoking the *A Clockwork Orange* sound world.

10:05 – We emerge into the finale and the re-introduction of the Elgar material, including a brief fairground waltz treatment of 'Land Of Hope And Glory' before the music begins to build to a hugely chaotic and dissonant climax. The piece concludes humorously with a backwards quotation from Richard Strauss's 'Also Sprach Zarathustra' (the fanfare music that opens Stanley Kubrick's film *2001: A Space Odyssey*).

Switched-On Brandenburgs (1980)

Personnel:
Wendy Carlos: Moog synthesizer, performance, arranging and engineering
Rachel Elkind: producer
Record label: Columbia Masterworks M2X 35895
Format: Double LP
Recorded at Elkind 'Brownstone' Studio, West 87th St, Manhattan
Release date: 1980
Highest chart position: US: 17 (*Billboard* Classical LPs)
Running time: 122:34

Switched-On Brandenburgs is a project in which Carlos realised the three remaining Bach Brandenburg Concertos of the six Concerto set (specifically numbers one, two and six), and in certain instances, reviewed and re-worked her earlier realisations. It marks the culmination of the analogue period of her synthesis work prior to her move into digital technologies (beginning with her hybrid score for the film *Tron* in 1982) and the apex of her explorations of Bach's music via the electronic medium. In its structure, the album also contrasts with the miscellaneous programmes of her earlier Baroque-music-themed recordings, now assembling a complete set of Bach's works on a single album under a unified theme. This, in effect, brought her work more into line with mainstream classical music recording practice, it being common, and even expected, for classical artists to produce integral surveys of a particular composer's work in a genre area such as the Symphony, Concerto or instrumental Sonata. At the same time, as with her previous *By Request* project, Carlos was also responding to her fanbase, as she commented in an interview with Dominic Milano for *Keyboard* magazine in December 1979:

We partially wanted to do it ourselves, and we got a lot of feedback from people who asked us to do a complete set. We used to include these funny little cards in our records that read, 'Please mail quickly'. It was even mentioned in a few reviews that it might be nice for this team to do the complete Brandies. Before, you had to go to different places and random selections of our records to hear them in incomplete form. Now, at least, there's an integral thing that contains our six Brandenburg realisations.

As the listener will already be aware from earlier discussions, a number of the works on this lavish two-disc LP (later CD) set appear on the following previously released records:

Brandenburg Concerto No. 2 First Movement (on *By Request*)
Brandenburg Concerto No. 3 (on *Switched-On Bach*)
Brandenburg Concerto No. 4 (on *The Well-Tempered Synthesizer*)
Brandenburg Concerto No. 5 (on *Switched-On Bach II*)

The third, fourth and fifth concertos were also given an interim compilation release in 1975 on *Bach: Brandenburg Concertos No. 3, 4 & 5: Virtuoso Electronic Performances Of Three Classics By Johann Sebastian Bach* (CBS S 73395). It is important to note, however, that there are both significant and subtle differences between the versions of the Concertos heard on these earlier recordings and *Switched-On Brandenburgs*, with some movements being reworked quite substantially. For example, the Second Movement of Brandenburg Concerto No. 3 – which it will be remembered had been treated to a rather unorthodox electronic interpretation for *Switched-On Bach* – has now been completely recomposed (Carlos also revisited this movement for a third time on *Switched-On Bach 2000*). Brandenburg Concerto No. 4, on the other hand, remains completely untouched. Hence, in the comments below, where the recording is identical, unless there are some significant differences in sound, mix etc, the listener will be directed to revisit the comments of previous chapters.

Concerto No. 1 In F Major
The first of the Brandenburg Concertos is particularly complex in its scoring and structure, which may explain why Carlos did not tackle it at an earlier stage in her career. Interestingly, it is the only Concerto with four movements, hence breaking out of the quick-slow-quick formula of the other works, the additional final movement being devised as a collection of dances, specifically a Minuet, two Trios and Polonaise. It also contains a wide variety of instrumentation, the soloists (the *concertino* group) consisting of two hunting horns, three oboes and a bassoon, which are accompanied by the usual strings and harpsichord continuo. This presented a challenge in synthesizing unique timbres that would work effectively both in isolation and in combination. The score also includes a *violino piccolo*, a small (later to become obsolete) violin tuned higher than the standard instrument, which has an important solo role in the second and third movements. Carlos did not like the sound of this instrument but, nonetheless, worked to create an authentic string timbre to remain faithful to Bach's conception, most notably in the second movement.

Allegro (4:10)
Carlos's realisation of the first movement is a precisely coordinated multi-track performance showing the usual attention to detail in her presentation of the music's individually characterful melodic strands. As we have observed with earlier Concerto settings, Carlos does not persistently employ the same sound each time a particular instrument re-appears; rather, her aim is to maintain a fluctuating tone colour scheme. This can be heard, for example, in the call-and-answer-like section from 2:18-3:08, which showcases a wide range of sounds, including a timbre that has an almost steel drum-like character. The hunting horns are also a memorable element of this movement

and have a strong presence in conventional orchestral performances. In response, Carlos has created an identifiable but relatively less obtrusive brass-like tone, which is certainly able to cut through the ensemble (e.g. in the opening group presentation of the *ritornello* material), although its sound is more easily appreciated in the sparser passages.

Adagio (4:06)

In this slow and mournful movement, the focus is pared down to two solo instruments – the first oboe and the violino piccolo – which play long-breathed and ornate melodies over a pulsing string accompaniment, underpinned by a prominent and pleasingly shaped bass line. In the beginning, the oboe and *violino piccolo* present individual solos, after which they then imitate and intertwine one another. Carlos's synthetic tone colours capture the sounds of these solo instruments very effectively, especially the *violino piccolo* line, which is convincingly string-like in its articulation.

Allegro (4:23)

In the jubilant Allegro, the *violino piccolo* steps forth as the main soloist, now performing material of a more virtuosic nature, although it tends not to be given the spotlight for very long. Carlos has again opted for a violin-like timbre which, if not as convincing as the slow movement, is nonetheless quite effective, capturing something of the character of the double-stops (chords played on the violin with a quick bowed motion) between 0:34-1:10. This is also a movement in which the horns again appear as a prominent element in Bach's scoring, including occasional exposure in solo lines. In this instance, however, a brass tone is largely absent from Carlos's chosen colour palette.

Menuetto; Trio I; Polacca; Trio II (6:51)

Carlos's liner notes indicate that she considerably altered the structure of Bach's additional fourth movement to reduce the role of the Menuetto (Minuet), which 'I've never particularly cared for', evoking the received scholarly view that Bach himself was quite flexible about how his works might be interpreted in different performance contexts. This means that in Bach's version, the Menuetto (the only one of the pieces to be scored for the full ensemble) is repeated after each of the dances, whereas in Carlos's version, it only returns once (without repeats) after Trio I. Carlos has also re-jigged the proceedings to give emphasis to the Polacca (Polonaise), originally scored for a small string group, which now frames the second Trio (on its later return, it is shortened by omitting the repeats). Trio I was scored by Bach for two oboes and bassoon; Carlos offers a synthesized version which is essentially imitative. In Trio II, Carlos's approach is to vary the orchestration of each repeated section, the first time around featuring synthesized horns accompanied by oboe-like timbres, the second time featuring synthesized horns accompanied by string-like timbres.

Concerto No. 2 In F Major

Carlos reveals in the LP's liner notes that her realisation of the second Concerto had been in development since the time of the soundtrack for *A Clockwork Orange*. However, only the first movement was completed to her and Elkind's satisfaction at this time, namely the version that appeared on *By Request*, and even this had problems (the continuo part) that still required a solution. Elkind, in fact, observes that Carlos only felt more confident in undertaking the remainder of Concerto No. 2 once she was able to create more convincing string-like timbres, using techniques developed while completing Concerto No. 1. This enabled her to more effectively handle the expressive solo instrument (violin and oboe) requirements of the second movement, although the results still remain far from naturalistic.

Allegro (5:48)

The Allegro movement of the Concerto has been updated for the LP to include a brand new continuo part played on the Electone E-5. This was remixed with the original multi-track used for *By Request*, and in Carlos's words, 'immediately changed the character of the movement'. The essential difference one encounters when comparing the first and second versions side by side (in addition to the lighter sound of the re-done continuo) is that the latter has an overall brighter (almost 'fizzy') presence, suggesting a favouring of the higher end in the mixing process. As a result, the solo instruments, particularly the high trumpet and recorder, now come through with greater clarity, highlighting the attention to detail given by Carlos to their emulation.

Andante (4:23)

This newly conceived realisation features some intriguing timbral experiments as Carlos explores the possibilities of expressivity in her execution of the oboe and violin parts (heard respectively in the left and right speakers). The resulting 'out-of-style wows' or 'electronic creepy-crawlies', as reviewers have variously referred to them, certainly remain an acquired taste for the Bach purist. Also quite unorthodox is the introduction of a white noise timbre (at 2:48), which is heard only for a few seconds, presumably included to add a little surface-level glitz. Overall, there is something of the spirit of Carlos, the experimental 'electronic' musician, in this movement, which one might have welcomed more of elsewhere. As Kenneth Cooper noted in his review of the LP in *High Fidelity* magazine (June 1980), 'it is where Carlos parts company with Bach that the proceedings really come to life'.

Allegro Assai (2:57)

The concluding Allegro Assai combines the fugue form with the *ritornello* structure and includes many long and exposed lines for the four solo instruments (trumpet, recorder, oboe and violin). Carlos's mix showcases each instrument with individual clarity, employing sounds that are, generally

Above: Carlos photographed alongside her Moog modular synthesizer, the instrument featured on *Switched-On Bach*. (*Alamy*)

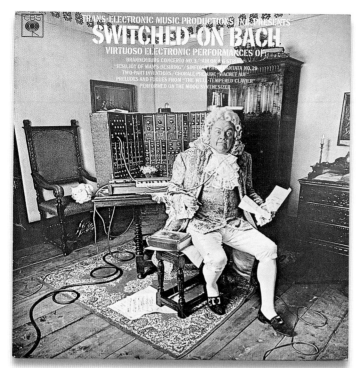

Left: The first *Switched-On Bach* cover features the notorious 'mugging' Bach and the disinterested cat. (*CBS*)

Right: The replacement *Switched-On Bach* cover, issued following Carlos's appeals to Columbia Records president Goddard Lieberson, features Bach in a somewhat more dignified pose with the cat unchanged. (*CBS*)

Right: The relatively futuristic cover for *The Well-Tempered Synthesizer* features likenesses of the four Baroque composers whose music appears on the LP. (*CBS*)

Trans-Electronic Music Productions, Inc. Presents

Walter Carlos

and

The Well-Tempered Synthesizer

More virtuoso electronic performances of Bach, Monteverdi, Scarlatti, Handel

STANLEY KUBRICK'S CLOCKWORK ORANGE

Left: The iconic artwork for the Warner Bros release of the soundtrack for *A Clockwork Orange*, the recording that influenced a generation of young electronic musicians. (*Warner Bros*)

Left: The distinctive mechanical clock cover for the alternative *A Clockwork Orange* soundtrack release – focused on Carlos's synthesizer music – evokes early 20th-century Dadaist collage style. (*CBS*)

Right: The front cover of the *Sonic Seasonings* double LP features part of the large multi-sectioned painting *Waves At Matsushima* by 17th-century Japanese Edo artist Ogata Kôrin. (*CBS*)

Right: 'One giant leap for synth-kind': Columbia's comical space-themed artwork for *Switched-On Bach II* conflates music technology with interplanetary travel. (*CBS*)

Left: The amusing cover of *By Request*, Carlos's first album to include synthesizer arrangements of popular music. (*CBS*)

Above: Robert A. Moog photographed around 1972, showing off his Moog modular synthesizer, Minimoog and Moog Sonic Six.

Below: A precocious young Carlos demonstrates her Audionics Project. (*Alamy*)

Right: This 1969 CBS advertisement for *Switched-On Bach* was typical of Columbia's marketing strategy to make synthesized classical music 'hip'.

Left: This 1969 Columbia Records advertisement for *The Well-Tempered Synthesizer* pokes fun at critics still unwilling to accept that classical music could be played on a synthesizer.

Left: *Switched-On Brandenburgs*: the orchestral machine is wired for sound in this captivating album artwork, which evokes the earlier woodcut tradition. (*CBS*)

Right: Here's Wendy! The much sought-after soundtrack for Stanley Kubrick's *The Shining* features two of Carlos's most widely recognized compositions. (*Warner Bros*)

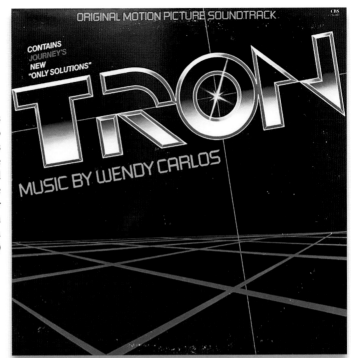

Right: Carlos's soundtrack to Disney's *Tron* was the first to feature digitally constructed sounds, alongside the Moog modular synthesizer, in combination with a live orchestra. (*CBS*)

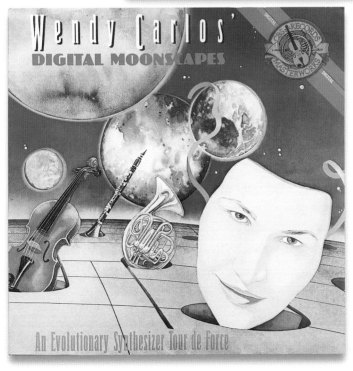

Left: Inspired by Holst's *The Planets*, Carlos dedicated her space-themed *Digital Moonscapes* album to NASA. (*CBS*)

Above: Carlos at the mixing console in Rachel Elkind's 'Brownstone' studio. (*Getty*)

Right: A 1976 Columbia advertisement for *By Request* announcing Carlos's new musical direction.

THE NEW MASTERWORKS ALBUM THAT GOES IN THE POP BIN: WALTER CARLOS—"BY REQUEST."

Since the release of "Switched-On Bach," sales of Walter Carlos product have totaled over 5,000,000 to cross-over audiences.

It's our Record of the Month—with every imaginable kind of special merchandising, advertising support in both print and radio, and a special low price.

And it includes a special seven-inch bonus record with excerpts from all six Carlos albums, to help you move that catalogue.

**Walter Carlos "By Request":
the Masterworks album that
belongs where 5,000,000
people can see it.
On Columbia Records =
and Tapes.**

Left: An advertisement for Carlos's *Tron* soundtrack issued ahead of the film's US release on 9 July 1982.

Left: The artwork for Carlos's *Beauty In The Beast* album reproduces a Balinese painting by W.Y. Weca, reflecting the Indonesian musical influence in the track 'Poem For Bali'. (*Audion/ East Side Digital/ Serendip*)

Right: Carlos's highly amusing musical collaboration with 'Weird Al' Yankovic on *Peter And The Wolf/Carnival Of The Animals – Part II* is unique in her recorded output. (*CBS*)

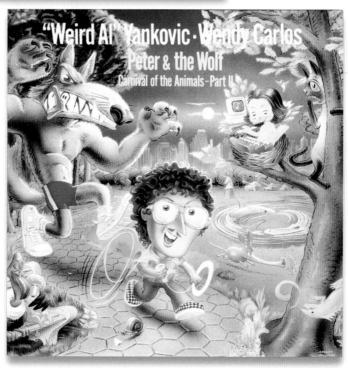

Right: With *Switched-On Bach 2000*, Carlos brings her original 1968 Bach concept fully into the domain of computerized music production. (*Telarc*)

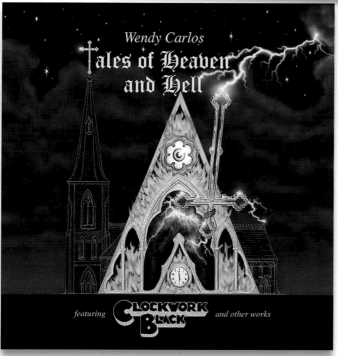

Left: Carlos's final unique album recording, *Tales Of Heaven And Hell* revisits her score for *A Clockwork Orange*, whose iconic artwork is also reimagined for its cover. (*East Side Digital/Serendip*)

Left: Hieronymus Bosch's *Visions Of The Hereafter*, reproduced on the reverse of *Tales Of Heaven And Hell*, may have been an inspiration for the track 'Seraphim'.

Above: One of Hieronymus Bosch's most famous paintings, *The Last Judgment* – partially reproduced on the reverse of *Tales Of Heaven And Hell* – provides an apt visual accompaniment to the album's centrepiece, 'Clockwork Black'.

Below: Carlos in her purpose-built West End Avenue studio around the time of *Switched-On Bach*.

Left and below: Front cover and first signed page of a limited print-run score of Carlos's composition 'Pompous Circumstances', which appears on the album *By Request*. (*Photograph of score from author's personal collection/Serendip*)

For this edition of

Pompous Circumstances

Two hundred copies have been printed by G. Schirmer, Inc. in Long Island, New York for Tempi Music, Inc.

This copy is signed by the composer.

This copy, number. 8

speaking, in accordance with Bach's original scoring, although, once again, the violin part is distinguished by the aforementioned 'out-of-style wows' (listen to the instrument in duo with the recorder part from 1:09, for example).

Concerto No. 3 In G Major
Allegro (6:26)
The original realisation of this movement, as heard on *Switched-On Bach*, is preserved essentially intact here. Hence, the earlier comments remain applicable.

Adagio (1:04)
For the second movement, Carlos took an opportunity to create a brand new (significantly shorter) realisation of Bach's sparsely notated score, having decided that the quirky experimental electronic approach she had employed on *Switched-On Bach* was now no longer appropriate. In the LP's liner notes, she explained why she had become dissatisfied with the original version:

> That sort of vocabulary is not at all consistent with that used in any of the other concertos – or even the rest of the Third. It was an attempt to show off the paraphernalia of the synthesizer in a way that perhaps needed to be done in 1968 but that is now not only redundant but also crude.

Instead, Carlos now opted to improvise at the keyboard in the style of Bach (the chosen timbre is harpsichord-like) over the two solitary chords that appear in the score. The resulting relatively simple music is further enhanced through the use of Carlos's hocketing technique, which, in her words, 'brings the recording to life in a way no standard performance can emulate'. Interestingly, the sheet music for this improvisation was reproduced in the gatefold for the 1980 LP (it also appears in the booklet for the 2001 ESD CD remaster) and is of interest because it includes bracketed indications for the placement of individual hocketed segments of the melody line within the stereo field. While less 'fun' than her original 1968 version, this realisation is, overall, more in keeping with a period-specific stylistic treatment of the Brandenburg Concertos in general terms.

Allegro (5:07)
The original realisation of this movement, as heard on *Switched-On Bach*, is preserved essentially intact here. Hence, the earlier comments remain applicable.

Concerto No. 4 In G Major
This Concerto is retained in its original version as heard on *The Well-Tempered Synthesizer*. This was simply because, as Carlos states in the LP's

65

liner notes, that realisation was 'one we've always liked'. The reader is thus referred to the earlier discussion of the piece for further information about the music and what to listen for (as a reminder, the movements are Allegro (8:02), Andante (3:35), Presto (4:39)).

Concerto No. 5 In D Major

Concerto No. 5 is essentially retained in the version released on *Switched-On Bach II* in 1973. As observed with the re-worked first movement of Brandenburg Concerto No. 2, there do appear to be some noticeable differences in the mixing and mastering, in practice impacting upon the emphasis and presence of certain sounds, but the recorded material is the same. This is hardly surprising given the complexity of Carlos's original realisation, in which she resolved particular issues of performance of the harpsichord part by recruiting the Electone E-5. Without a complete overhaul, it would be hard to imagine what she could have done to further advance her interpretation. The reader is thus referred to the earlier discussion of the piece for further information about the music and what to listen for (as a reminder, the movements are Allegro (10:47), Affetuoso (5:31) and Allegro (4:48)).

Concerto No. 6 In B Flat Major

The sixth concerto, the last to be completed for the LP, was a work that Carlos found to be more challenging to realise on account of Bach's orchestra being partly made up of instruments of the viol family (early bowed string instruments that were fretted like guitars), including the viola da braccio (x 2) and the viola da gamba (x 2). This produced an emphasis on the lower range, creating a thickness which Carlos found to be 'very murky', necessitating some clever re-scoring to thin it out. According to Carlos's new notes for the ESD re-release, her realisation also makes extensive use of the Electone E-5 organ previously encountered on *Switched-On Bach II*, which, once again, is co-opted to solve the problem of rendering the fluid harpsichord solo parts convincingly. In the LP liner notes, Carlos comments that the realisation of the continuo part was, in fact, the most adventurous part of the album, characterised by 'strange little arpeggios and spatial movements'.

Allegro (6:53)

Musically, this movement is notable for its use of canon (a technique in which one instrumental part is immediately imitated by another) in the upper voices throughout, underpinned by a continuously chugging rhythmic accompaniment. The canonic aspect of the music is much enhanced in Carlos's treatment by the wide spectrum of synthesizer colours employed with touch sensitivity, the careful call-and-response style arrangement of the parts within the stereo field and the use of spatial effects (listen from 3:11-3:46 and 5:35-5:58, for example, to appreciate this). On the whole, this is a compelling and expressive re-imagining which breathes new life into the Bach original, the overall bright sound of Carlos's enhanced orchestration conveying the essential detail of the music in ways that would have been impossible for an 18th-century listener.

Adagio Ma Non Tanto (4:37)
As is typical of the Brandenburg slow movements, the instrumental forces are once again reduced, in this case, to the two viola da braccio soloists, a 'walking' cello bass and continuo accompaniment. Compared to the first movement, Bach's music now has a more complex contrapuntal character, featuring a long fugue-like main theme whose development is shared by the solo instruments, giving the effect of a musical conversation. Carlos employs an expressive, string-like timbre for the viola da braccio, positioning the two soloists in the left and right speakers and varying the tonal character using oscillator and filter envelope modulation. The expressivity is further enhanced by the dramatic swells of volume that occur on many of the phrases.

Allegro (5:29)
A standout aspect of this buoyant and tuneful concluding Allegro is Carlos's now very familiar hocketing technique, enhanced by some interjected reverberation effects which give the impression of the music being situated in a large hall. As in the first movement, we have a wonderful panoply of bright, sharp-edged tones, which give a pointedness to the fast-running rhythms.

The Shining (1980)

Personnel:
Wendy Carlos: Moog synthesizer, Circon, performance and arranging
Rachel Elkind: vocal performances and production
Record label: Warner Bros WB 56827
Format: LP
Recorded at Elkind 'Brownstone' Studio, West 87th St, Manhattan and London
Release date: 1980
Highest chart position: N/A
Running time: 6:28 (Carlos tracks only)

The original soundtrack for Stanley Kubrick's film *The Shining* was given its first release on LP in 1980. However, the recording quickly went out of print due to licensing issues concerning the copyrighted (mainly) contemporary music that appears on the album. Carlos and Elkind were asked to contribute original music for the soundtrack, initially working from the Stephen King novel rather than the completed (and rather different) film, and developed a large number of musical cues (self-contained pieces tailored to specific scenes) that were closely allied with the script. Disappointingly for Carlos, with the exception of two compositions, 'The Shining' and 'Rocky Mountains', the vast majority of this music was ultimately rejected by Kubrick, who instead opted to derive the bulk of the soundtrack from pre-existing avant-garde pieces by Eastern European modernist composers, including Béla Bartók, Krystof Penderecki and György Ligeti (the latter's music already having featured in *2001: A Space Odyssey*). While *The Shining* LP thus does not strictly count as a wholly 'Carlos' album, it has, nevertheless, become known as a seminal Carlos recording, and indeed, the two Carlos compositions that made the final cut still represent, for many, the essential music of the soundtrack. Both were used by Kubrick to accompany scenes early in the film, hence playing a key role in shaping its mood and have become inextricably entwined with the breathtaking cinematographic sequences that are themselves the stuff of legend. It should be noted that Carlos's complete score for *The Shining* eventually received a full release on her two-volume compilation CD *Rediscovering Lost Scores*, issued on the East Side Digital label in 2005 (see the later discussion in the 'Miscellaneous, Compilations, Curiosities And Rarities' section).

'The Shining' (3:27)

Carlos's music for the iconic opening scene of the film makes prominent use of the 'Dies Irae', an ancient melody which, as already observed, first appeared in a more subtle manner in Carlos's soundtrack for her first Kubrick film *A Clockwork Orange*. In an interview for Vincent LoBrutto's 1997 biography of Kubrick, Carlos explains how she brought the melody to the director's attention:

When we were in London, Stanley wanted to know if there was anything I could think of that would apply to music about graves, death and ghosts. I suggested Dies Irae, which is, of course, part of the Latin requiem mass. It always haunted me the way it haunted Rachmaninoff, like it haunted Ravel, like it haunted Berlioz. Kubrick asked me to think of a place where you could hear it, and I said, 'Well, there are some archive recordings that have the real Gregorian chants'. So, I suggested the Berlioz Requiem. I told him to listen to the last movement. He got the record and he must have played it a hundred times or more and he got very wedded to it.

Carlos's music functions as the film's 'main title' and accompanies the sequence which follows Jack Torrance's car on its first journey through the Rocky Mountains to the Overlook Hotel. Kubrick's stunning presentation of the natural environment, which is shot from a helicopter swooping across the landscape, is matched by the grandiosity of Carlos's cue. The unaccompanied 'Dies Irae' tune initially dominates the music in a dramatic and foreboding manner. It is presented twice in the lower register using a brass-like timbre on the Moog (Carlos states that this was a combination of tuba and bassoon sounds), which has been filtered to remove much of its high-frequency content, creating a claustrophobic effect. The contrasting centrepiece is an electronic soundscape comprising a drone-like texture over which we hear wordless vocal sounds performed by Elkind, treated to reverb and delay effects. This is highly evocative music which suggests the calls of unnamed creatures (or perhaps demonic spirits, in reference to the ancient Indian burial ground on which the Overlook Hotel is built) echoing around the mountains. Another interesting element of Carlos's sound design in this section is her use of an autoharp, a metal-stringed zither-like instrument whose strings are scraped with a plectrum.

'Rocky Mountains' (3:01)

Carlos's second cue (accompanying the Torrance family's journey through the Rocky Mountains to the Overlook Hotel) is built on a rich brass timbre. The deep tones Carlos employs here, in particular, call to mind the opening music of Richard Wagner's *Das Rheingold* (from the Ring cycle), which uses similar low brass sounds to suggest the primordial character of the Rhine. Much of the music of this cue is drone-like and is characterised by the use of glissandos, meaning that individually sustained lines are frequently pitched up and down by tiny gradations. Carlos states in her notes for the first volume of *Rediscovering Lost Scores* that she achieved this effect using an instrument she had built herself called the Circon (short for Circular Controller), which sounds similar to a Theremin (a demonstration of this device by Carlos can be found in a short clip on the 'Special Features' disc of the 2008 Special Edition DVD of the film). The resultant fluid textures and dissonant combinations (again enhanced by long tape delay effects) are ultimately well aligned with the Eastern European pieces that comprise the main part of the film's soundtrack, the 'Rocky Mountains' cue segueing quite naturally into the Ligeti piece ('Lontano') which follows.

Tron (1982)

Personnel:
Wendy Carlos: GDS and Moog Synthesizers, performance and arranging
Annemarie Franklin: assistant to the composer
London Philharmonic Orchestra conducted by Douglas Gamley
Martin Neery: Royal Albert Hall Organ
UCLA Chorus directed by Donn Weiss
Jorge Calandrelli: orchestrations
Record label: CBS Records 70223
Format: LP
Recorded at Carlos' Loft studio, Greenwich Village, New York and London
(Royal Albert Hall and Walthamstow Hall)
Release date: 9 July 1982
Highest chart position: US: 135 (*Billboard* 200)
Running time: 49:41

Carlos's soundtrack for the Disney film *Tron* signals her move into the field
of digital synthesis, ushering in a new sonic identity that she was to build
upon in subsequent albums during the 1980s, including *Digital Moonscapes*
and *Beauty In The Beast*. Moreover, as the first LP of original music by Carlos
since 1972's *Sonic Seasonings*, it served to re-establish her in the public eye as
a composer of great range and versatility. A key element of the sound of the
Tron score is the Italian-made Crumar GDS (the letters standing for General
Development System) Matrix Synthesizer, which Carlos acquired in 1981.
The GDS, created by Hal Alles of Bell Labs, was an 'additive' synthesizer,
meaning that it employed the same synthesis principles as the Hammond
organ, in which a tone colour is gradually built up by combining pure sine
waves, the sounds in this instance being digitally synthesised (using computer
chips) rather than being produced by electricity moving in circuitry. As such,
this new technology presented exciting new possibilities for sound design,
enabling Carlos to dramatically expand her colour palette – as she states in
her liner notes for the 2001 re-release of the soundtrack, it was the GDS that
was responsible for the 'wild organic sounds' heard in the score (some of
which are highlighted in the commentary below, such as 'Tower Music' and
'A New Tron And The MCP'). Interestingly, the *Tron* score also integrates the
GDS with Carlos's trusty Moog, allowing her to bring her earlier synthesizer
aesthetic into play with the new sound world, resulting in a rather unusual
digital-analogue melange. Furthermore, both synthesizers are combined with
a live orchestra and choir, making the score a unique hybrid of electronically
generated and acoustic sounds that was pioneering for the time. Where the
music's relationship with the film was concerned, Carlos's new technological
aesthetic also cohered well with the equally progressive CGI techniques
employed in the making of *Tron*, which juxtaposes the real world with an
artificial one inside a computer, marrying live action with synthetic visuals to

produce a novel cinematic experience. According to Carlos's later liner notes, the plan had initially been to use her electronically conceived music to suggest the internal computer environment while reserving the more conventional orchestral music for the real-world scenes. However, this was ultimately abandoned in favour of a score which fused the two perspectives throughout.

In musical terms, *Tron* showcases the wide scope of Carlos's compositional ability and the range of classical music influences that had shaped her musical style to this point, including 20th-century composers, such as Claude Debussy, Igor Stravinsky, György Ligeti and Krzysztof Penderecki. Compared to *Sonic Seasonings,* which combined found sound recordings with synthetic textures, we are now in relatively 'traditional' territory in that this is, for the most part, conventionally scored orchestral/choral music with occasional forays into more abstract electronic music conceptions. As with many traditional orchestral film scores, the soundtrack is built from a series of cues that are, in essence, mini-variations in different musical and instrumental guises of a distinctive (and malleable) theme, in this case, the three-note idea introduced in the opening music 'Creation Of Tron'. This technique is something of a departure for Carlos, whose previous film soundtrack for *A Clockwork Orange* was based on standalone arrangements of classical works, which did not allow for overall thematic integration. While this approach sat well with Kubrick, it did not suit the Disney context, which required original music tailored to the needs of the narrative. There is a sense in this score that Carlos is responding directly to aspects of the classic Disney music style, particularly in her use of angelic-sounding choirs (think of films such as *Snow White* or *Bambi*, for example), which underline the religious subtext of the film. In contrast to the Disney aesthetic, however, Carlos's musical language is often rapidly changeable, the various generally short cues juxtaposing a wide range of contrasting musical moods, from the dissonant and jarring to the repetitive and rhythmically strident to the contemplative and sentimental.

'Creation Of Tron' (0:45)

This short piece accompanies the film's opening sequence, in which the figure of Tron is gradually pieced together from fragments, which coalesce in the centre of the screen. It is the first of several occasions in the score in which Carlos uses the choir, which introduces the soundtrack's main three-note 'Tron' motif with a dramatic flourish. This idea will be reworked in numerous ways as the soundtrack develops, eventually forming the basis of the 'Theme From Tron' melody.

'Only Solutions' (3:15) (Jonathan Cain, Steve Perry and Neal Schon)

'Only Solutions' is the film's signature pop song (the title taken from a line spoken by Flynn), performed by the multi-platinum rock band Journey. It is used as background music at Flynn's arcade early on in the film and then reappears complete in the final credits, at which point it usurps time from

Carlos's own 'Ending Titles' music. While Carlos had previously undertaken work in the popular music sphere (see *Childe Harold* later in this book), she was not involved in writing this song, which, in musical terms, bears no connection with the *Tron* score itself. 'Only Solutions' was also released as a 45-rpm (CBS AE7 1530) single backed by Carlos's 'Theme From Tron'.

'We've Got Company' (2:15)

The title of this track refers to a line spoken by Flynn prior to one of the film's first video-game-like action scenes. In this cue, the three-note theme, previously introduced by the choir in 'Creation Of Tron', now returns in a rather different musical setting. The music opens with a dramatic orchestral crescendo, capped by a powerful statement in the brass section before we are launched headlong into the synthesizer/orchestra sound world of the *Tron* score. After a glissando (sliding) effect on the strings (a device drawn from avant-garde classical music), there is a longer section of music of a more rhythmic character, characterised by punctuating jabs in the strings and interjections from other synthetic and orchestral sounds, during the course of which we hear further statements of the 'Creation Of Tron' theme. The music reaches a climax at 1:42 and then gives way to a shimmering texture of strings and harp, leading to a final crescendo.

'Wormhole' (2:25)

This music accompanies the sequence in which the film's main character Flynn is transplanted from the real world into the electronic computer environment. A dissonant opening chord immediately establishes a mood of tension, which builds to a loud trumpet motif (a quotation of a famous musical phrase from Stravinsky's ballet *The Rite Of Spring*) at 0:22, accompanied by frenetic string music. After a minute, the music becomes more subdued and sustained as the electronic world is gradually revealed in all its majesty before building to another crescendo (including an effective use of choir) and then dissolving into a slow descending glissando.

'Ring Game And Escape' (2:53)

This music accompanies the famous one-on-one duel between Flynn and Crom on the Game Grid. The militaristic drumming music heard at the beginning of this cue establishes the martial mood of the scene. We hear stabbed, slightly off-tune synthesizer chords, which appear to imitate the percussive rhythms. Subsequently, the 'Creation Of Tron' theme is re-introduced, becoming a unifying element of the music which follows. The music section from 1:16 onwards refers to the scene in which Flynn, Tron and Ram use their light cycles to escape from the evil Sark and the Game Tanks. After a moment of repose, the militaristic drumming returns, leading to the appearance of a new melody, which becomes a prominent feature of the escape music until the end.

73

'Water, Music And Tronaction' (2:36)

This cue demonstrates Carlos's ability to write music of a mysterious, almost ethereal character, providing a backdrop to the scene in which the three fugitives stop to refresh themselves in a stream of liquid power. The music, evoking the stream, is calm in character, based on a repeating pattern delicately orchestrated in the higher register and featuring light bell-like percussion. Over this pattern, we hear the three-note Tron motif and intimations of the way in which it will later be reworked as the 'Theme From Tron'. The angelic choir is also used here to suggest a quasi-religious dimension to the characters' rejuvenation by the (holy) stream of water. From 1:29 (the 'Tronaction' section), the music becomes more agitated as the characters once again begin to be pursued by the Game Tanks.

'Tron Scherzo' (1:43)

In describing this short number as a Scherzo (meaning 'joke'), a fast piece with a feel of 3/4 time, Carlos reminds us of her use of Beethoven's music in the score for *A Clockwork Orange*. It is a lively cue of a dance-like character, which begins with a strident, widely spaced, fanfare-like phrase employing a familiar brass-like synthesizer tone, which is punctuated by heavy chords. The music then becomes fuller textured and rhythmically forthright as this theme is developed. Following this, we move into a quieter and more subdued section, dominated by a new repetitive melodic idea (suggestive in its design of minimalist music), which has an irregular phrase structure. This recedes into the background as an electronically generated, slow-descending glissando appears to pull the music ever downwards (the effect is of a machine running out of power).

'Miracle And Magician' (2:36)

This music accompanies the scene in which Flynn discovers he has unique powers of rejuvenation in the computer world that none of his electronic counterparts possess. The first part of the cue employs the three-note 'Creation Of Tron' theme in a fanfare-like manner, followed by a series of chords that evoke a state of wonder. The cue's development after this point then follows the changing action, with music that is, at first, more agitated and then of a restful and sentimental character, with the 'Creation Of Tron' motif functioning as a recurrent element.

'Magic Landings' (3:40)

This music accompanies Flynn's journey across the Electronic World in his commandeered enemy craft. Much of the piece is based on a continuous repeating 'oom-pah' style (in an irregular seven beats to the bar) accompanying pattern, which imparts a generally more light-hearted, even humorous character (reflecting Flynn's struggles to pilot the craft and land it safely). Again, we hear the three-note Tron motif, as well as a longer melody we first encountered in the 'Escape' sequence.

'Theme From Tron' (1:30)

This slower, gentler music, combining synthetic and conventional acoustic string sounds, is in a contrasting 'romantic' musical style, allowing for some respite from the preceding tensions. The basis of this piece is the three-note Tron theme, which is now extended and elaborated to produce a lyrical and emotionally expressive melody that occupies a 7/4 time signature. The original Tron motif is thus reincarnated as a new thematic idea that becomes an important feature of later cues in the soundtrack.

'1990's Theme' (2:25) (Jonathan Cain and Neal Schon)

The second contribution to the LP by Journey offers a futuristic vision of 1990s pop (*Tron* is set in the 1980s), which, perhaps thankfully, did not materialise! The track functions diegetically (in other words, it is part of the film's own world) as background music to the first scene at Flynn's Arcade. Neal Schon's lead guitar is the main melodic focus here, playing a simple repeated hook accompanied by a pounding drum beat, bass guitar and synthesizer sweeps, the latter probably performed by Carlos.

'Love Theme' (2:03)

A gorgeous shimmering string texture opens the cue, over which is heard a simple melodic phrase. The choir, once again, produce an ethereal harmony, accompanied by snippets of music that are reminiscent of the 'Water' theme, after which we hear fragments of the original three-note Tron motif, which morphs into the longer melody of the 'Theme From Tron' (beautifully scored for solo string instruments). An emotive vocal/orchestral passage follows, heralding further restatements of this theme as the music builds to a breathtaking conclusion.

'Tower Music – Let Us Pray' (3:43)

The GDS synthesiser was presumably the source of the abstract electronic sounds created for the first section of this foreboding piece ('Tower Music'), whose style is reminiscent, in some ways, of the experimental textures of 'Timesteps' on *A Clockwork Orange*. At 1:33 (the 'Let Us Pray' section), this mood gives way to a more tranquil musical setting characterised by washes of chord colour, after which a brass motif is heard accompanied by wordless choral harmonies. A slow ascending glissando at 2:25 leads into a new passage of music composed to accompany the sequence in which Tron receives enlightenment in the Tower. This moves through a series of short repeating figures, vocal stabs and alternating chords, eventually alighting on the 'Theme From Tron' melody at its conclusion.

'The Light Sailer' (2:32)

The title of this piece refers to the dragonfly-like 'Solar Sailer', the flying craft that the film's protagonists use to escape from Game Grid and locate the Master Control Program (the 'villain' of the film). Carlos's music here is dramatic in character to suit the scene, which documents the battle to launch the craft and maintain course. The cue opens with lovely, rich, sustained synthesizer chords before we move into a more rhythmic section, which reprises the 'Tron Scherzo' material, as well as the 'Escape' music.

'Sea Of Simulation' (3:20)

The piece begins with music of a dance-like character (the 'oom pah' feel is once again prominent), eventually giving way to dissonant stabbing string chords (rather like Bernard Hermann's *Psycho* motif). During this section, we hear occasional interjections of the three-note Tron theme. There is then a brief period of respite as the music becomes more fragmentary before the sprightly repeating melody heard in 'Tron Scherzo' is re-introduced in the higher register, accompanied by a low bass part. This leads, after a short period, to a passage of sustained music until a further statement of the Tron theme triggers the return of the 'Tron Scherzo' idea in a fuller-sounding instrumental guise, building to a dramatic climax.

'A New Tron And The MCP' (5:45)

The title refers to the culmination of the film's action as the heroes finally destroy the evil MCP and establish a benign replacement. One of the longest and most impressive cues of the soundtrack, this is a piece in which the electronic elements (heard at the outset and then later at intervals) showcase the sound design possibilities of the GDS synthesizer. The first part of the piece is of an abstract, electronic character, Carlos's innovative textures gradually being joined by the orchestra and synthesizers and building gradually to a forceful brass-led crescendo overlaid by the choir. The section of orchestral/electronic music from 2:00-3.23 is particularly inventive, employing the orchestra in a manner which owes something to the influence of 1960s avant-garde composers such as Ligeti and Penderecki (whose music Carlos would probably have absorbed via Kubrick's scores). At 3:41, we hear the 'Theme From Tron' in an epic choral setting, but this is soon cut short at 4:03 as the dark electronic atmospheres return to conclude the piece (suggesting the MCP's destruction) in a sequence which is certainly one of the most remarkable of the entire score.

'Anthem' (1:36)

'Anthem' is a short, celebratory cue which evokes the sense of triumph of good over evil following the destruction of the MCP and the transformation of the Electronic World. The first part of the piece is a reprise of the 'Theme From Tron' in which the choir features as a prominent element. From 1:00, the mood changes as a pulsating rhythm re-introduces the 'Wormhole' music, which then builds to a dissonant climax to underscore Flynn's return to the real world.

'Ending Titles' (5:10)

The second of the two longer cues on the soundtrack, this music is heard as the final credits roll. While the director chose to use only the first 3 minutes of Carlos's piece in order to carve out the space for the inclusion of Journey's 'Only Solutions' in the film, the soundtrack LP features the entire composition as Carlos intended it to be heard (the 20th Anniversary Collector's Edition DVD of the film also has an option to listen to the complete score over the credits, minus the Journey song). Hearing the piece in its entirety allows one to appreciate the music's three-part structure, which begins with an orchestral reprise of the melodic material heard in 'Theme From Tron' and 'Anthem', now clothed in a variety of instrumental colours, eventually being joined by the angelic choirs. From 1:38, this material is then reworked as an organ solo (here played with great expression by Martin Neery on the Royal Albert Hall organ). The final section (from 2:55) returns to the more frenetic music of the kind heard in tracks such as 'We've Got Company' and 'Ring Game And Escape'.

Digital Moonscapes (1984)

Personnel:

Wendy Carlos: GDS and Synergy Synthesizers, performance, arranging, recording and production

Annemarie Franklin: notes compiling and editing/logistical support

Record label: CBS Masterworks M39340

Format: LP/CD

Recorded at Carlos's Loft studio, Greenwich Village, New York

Release date: August 1984

Highest chart position: US: 33 (*Billboard* Top Classical Albums)

Running time: 55:38

Digital Moonscapes is a concept album whose theme is astronomy and whose musical framing is, unsurprisingly for Carlos, a classical one. The album comprises two suites (a suite is a collection of related pieces), respectively entitled 'Cosmological Impressions' and 'Moonscapes' (focusing on the moons of four planets: Earth, Mars, Jupiter and Saturn). Each of the pieces has a programmatic title – in other words, one which refers to the astronomical or planetary subject matter which inspired the composition and which the music is intended to, in some way, suggest or portray. Carlos's liner notes indicate that a particular influence on 'Moonscapes' is the famous orchestral suite *The Planets* (1916) by Gustav Holst, a work that had itself recently been treated to two imaginative electronic re-imaginings by Japanese synthesizer pioneer Isao Tomita (*The Planets*) and American electronic musician Patrick Gleeson (*Beyond The Sun*), both released in 1976. Interestingly, Gleeson's superb realisation (using an Eu Systems polyphonic synthesizer) received strong approbation from Carlos herself, who contributed an extended sleeve note for the LP. The music of *Digital Moonscapes* is as advanced as anything Carlos had previously attempted on earlier albums, if not more so. For example, her handling of thematic material and musical forms remains highly sophisticated, while the musical language itself is often of a decidedly abstract character on account of her experimenting with polytonality (multiple keys combined) and irregular rhythmic juxtapositions of time signatures and metre.

Described on the LP cover as 'An Evolutionary Synthesizer Tour de force', *Digital Moonscapes* is also of interest from a technological perspective, marking a further advance in the digital synthesis experiments begun on *Tron*. In addition to her Crumar GDS unit, Carlos employed two recently purchased Synergy digital additive synthesizers (again built by Crumar, now operating under the name Digital Keyboards), which afforded yet more flexibility in the creation and control of sounds. Among the revolutionary (for the time) features of the Synergy was the ability to quickly morph in real-time between different timbres across the keyboard and an on-board sequencer, which allowed for the more convenient programming and overdubbing of recorded parts. Carlos was thus rapidly moving further and further away from the relatively cumbersome and painstaking approach to constructing sounds on her Moog and rendering them to tape in a 'take-by-take' fashion that had been at the heart of her work during the 1970s. These developments naturally had a marked impact on both the sonic character of Carlos's music and its execution in performance. Furthermore, *Digital Moonscapes* is also Carlos's first digital recording, the performances being captured with a then state-of-the-art Sony PCM F-1 Portable Digital Audio Recorder, and also her first release on the relatively recently developed Compact Disc format (alongside the usual vinyl LP). Therefore, digital technologies were now adding additional levels of mediation to the sound quality at each stage of the production process, resulting in a marked qualitative difference in the audio result.

Carlos's liner notes convey her excitement at the developments in digital synthesis technology she was exploring at this time, indicating that she had been waiting for this moment since *Switched-On Bach*. Her comments reveal that she had, in fact, long been dissatisfied with the possibilities of analogue synthesis on the Moog due to the limitations of its tonal palette and the impossibility of achieving realistic renderings of orchestral sounds. Digital synthesis, however, was at last making it possible for her to achieve her aim of emulating real orchestral instruments with high accuracy. As such, Carlos developed, in her words, 'the world's first digitally synthesised orchestra', which she dubbed the LSI Philharmonic (possibly a pun on the London Symphonic Orchestra), the letters standing for 'Large Scale Integration' in reference to the role that computer chips were now playing in the creation of her sounds. This will no doubt come as a surprise to most readers, who would hardly have viewed the sound palette that Carlos developed for the Moog as limited! Indeed, it was arguably the uniquely 'unreal' quality of the tone colours she produced using the synthesizer that had given her re-imaginings of Bach their distinctive character. However, although Carlos appeared to be now rejecting analogue synthesis as something relatively primitive, it is clear from her comments that she remained open-minded and regarded digital synthesis in the same way that she had analogue synthesis in 1968: as a new frontier of sonic exploration in which the technology was a means to 'build new sounds with orchestral qualities that have not been heard before'. In an interview for *Downbeat* magazine in March 1987, Carlos summed up her strategy for creating *Digital Moonscapes*:

For me, the *Digital Moonscapes* record was my testimony to saying, 'look at how close the technology allows a very obsessive person to get to the symphonic tradition's sounds', you know – the acoustical wealth of riches that were polished by the Steinways, the Stradivarians, the Guarneri family, the Boehms and all these other people who built the marvellous instruments that make up a fine orchestra. And while I don't pretend for a moment to have duplicated – that would be an insult – I think, nevertheless, the word replicate is a decent enough compromise, in terms of terminology, to suggest that I feel I have gotten the essence of what it is that makes that sound appealing to us without quite duplicating it.

The LP was, on the whole, well-received by critics, who were particularly impressed by Carlos's achievements in the realm of digital synthesis. Edward Tatnall Canby of *Audio* magazine wrote in October 1985, for example, that:

There is no doubt of the truth in this record's subtitle, An Evolutionary Synthesizer Tour de Force. I put the record on my table without even glancing at the fancy annotations and was very quickly aware of the new subtlety and expressiveness of these synthesized sounds, mostly suggesting acoustic orchestral equivalents. Definitely ahead of anything I had heretofore sampled ... Carlos has been an important and knowledgeable force in moving synthesized sound away from the oversimplifications of waveform and scope that we know so well into – via digital – a new subtlety that is astonishing. Yes, one can now create strings, horns, woodwinds and any old sounds, not to mention unnamed ones, that have the pulsing, living quality of 'real' or acoustic sound.

Cosmological Impressions

In the first shorter suite of pieces, 'Cosmological Impressions', Carlos implies in her main title and the names 'Genesis' and 'Eden' that she is conflating biblical references with the emergence of the universe. Her use of the word 'impressions' in the title also suggests musical impressionism of the kind associated with composers such as Claude Debussy, as well as the work of late 19th-century French painters such as Monet and Renoir. To put it another way, these are musical portraits whose individual titles imply that each composition will be in some way suggestive of something associated with them, thereby conditioning the listening experience.

'Genesis' (7:10)

As the title indicates through its reference to the first book of the Old Testament, the music here is intended to suggest the gradual formation of the universe from the void. It does this through a slow and progressive build-up of elements, beginning with string-like sustained notes, whose 'cold' digital timbres appear highly appropriate in suggesting the emptiness of space. These sustained notes begin to overlap and are overlaid with arabesque-like figures clothed in woodwind-like timbres, which indicate growing signs of life. From around 2:51, this gradually coalesces into a more active rhythmic motion and subsequently evolves into a captivating section of music, in which a long-breathed melody is accompanied by scintillating arpeggios (Carlos states that the theme heard at this point represents the 'dawn of life'). There is a culminating pipe organ-like chord at 5:29, which appears to mark a point of arrival as the full majesty of the universe is revealed, the music eventually ending calmly on a sustained chord which fades out.

'Eden' (4:25)
The construction of this piece, consisting of 'three main themes and three sub-themes', which are carefully combined into a contrapuntal texture, reminds one that Carlos is a composer deeply steeped in Baroque musical forms. Her themes here are simply melodic, almost folk-like in fact, and her strategy is similar to 'Genesis' in that there is a gradual process of building up this material instrumentally to a grand climax. The music is orchestrated using synthesized sounds that are clearly intended to emulate familiar instruments, including string, woodwind and brass instruments.

'I.C. (Intergalactic Communications)' (3:40)
One of the most accessible and enjoyable pieces on the LP, 'Intergalactic Communications' suggests the influence of American minimalist music of composers such as Steve Reich, Terry Riley and especially Philip Glass, whose popular *Glassworks* LP had been released two years earlier. Typical of this genre, the music is built from simple musical phrases that repeat unchanged throughout, the strategy being to sustain interest by introducing new elements at periodic intervals. In this instance, there are two main contrasting ideas, one of a busy rhythmic character, the other slower and more lyrical, over which are overlaid a number of sub-melodic and rhythmic elements utilising a variety of contrasting tone colours. A built-in feature which prevents the music from becoming overly predictable is Carlos's choice to use an irregular 13/8 time signature!

Moonscapes
The *Digital Moonscapes* LP contains an attractive gatefold showing photographs of the various moons which inspired the *Moonscapes* suite, alongside brief programme notes by Carlos. The comments below are intended to supplement these notes while drawing attention to musical elements of interest.

'Luna' (8:15)
The first movement of the suite (and its longest) is a homage to Earth's own moon, with Carlos drawing upon particular opposing characteristics – namely 'love' and 'lunacy' – for musical inspiration. This idea, in effect, determines the highly changeable (what Carlos calls 'schizophrenic') character of the music, which moves through a number of moods and thematic personalities. Instrumental tone colours frequently come and go in this piece (facilitated by the Synergy's mapping capabilities), showcasing the full range of Carlos's digital sound design palette, and there are frequent alternations between the dramatic orchestral presentation of the main themes (e.g. 0:00-1:13 and

2:54) and more thinly textured passages (e.g. 3:01- 3:25) in which specific solo instrumental sounds can be clearly perceived. Of note is the lyrical and thickly textured romantic music heard between 1:15-2:46 (and later at 4:46-5:31), which features a lead instrument that is rather saxophone-like in character.

'Phobos And Deimos' (3:25)

The second piece portrays Phobos and Deimos, the two moons of Mars, which are known for their distinctively misshapen quality (Phobos has a strange potato-like appearance, for example). Carlos's liner notes give a sense of her aims in musically emulating these moons, which she describes as fast-moving and physiognomically 'the least attractive' in the solar system. This interpretation is borne out in her rather agitated and often comical musical setting, which is characterised by jaunty dance-like phrases (reflecting the influence of the Scherzo perhaps), pounding rhythms, growling, low brass-like timbres, rapid crescendos and sudden interjections. Each of the moons has its own theme, the one allocated to Phobos (a syncopated exchange between horn and trombone) first appearing at 0:13-0:33 and that of Deimos (a flowing gigue-like tune over a monotonous stabbed rhythm) at 0:33-1:03. At times, there are strong reminiscences of Carlos's score for *Tron*, which is unsurprising given that this material would still have been fresh in her mind.

'Ganymede' (4:22)

The relatively calm and measured musical setting of Ganymede (Jupiter's largest moon) provides much-needed relief from the frenetic sound world of 'Phobos And Deimos'. Perhaps inspired by Kubrick's use of Johann Strauss II's 'Blue Danube' in *2001: A Space Odyssey*, Carlos has set the music in 3/4 time as a waltz (according to Carlos, specifically a 'jazz waltz'), which imparts a graceful character to the music. However, Carlos comments that she has employed a ten-bar chord progression (this can be clearly heard in a brass-like voicing from 0:40-0:55), which imparts a certain asymmetrical unpredictability to the phrasing. As with 'Luna', we are treated to a wide range of instrumental colours here, which are used to distinguish the music's various primary and subsidiary themes.

'Europa' (4:17)

The fourth movement of the *Moonscapes* suite, the second to be inspired by a satellite of Jupiter, is of a more subdued and contemplative nature. Here, Carlos provides an atmospheric musical imagining of Europa's unchanging icy surface, using a repeating two-chord pattern to produce an effect of stasis. As such, Carlos once again reveals the influence of Claude Debussy on her music, bringing to mind his impressionistic piano pieces such as 'Des Pas Sur Le Neige' ('Footsteps In The Snow'), which conjure up compelling sound pictures of natural phenomena. Arthur C. Clarke's description of an imagined landing on Europa in his 1982 book *2010: Odyssey Two* (which is referred to by Carlos in her liner notes) offers an evocative description of the character of this moon and is worth quoting for the benefit of the listener:

> That ice was flat from pole to pole; there was no weather to carve it into strange shapes, no drifting snow to build up layer upon layer into slowly moving hills. Meteorites might fall upon airless Europa, but never a flake of snow. The only forces moulding its surface were the steady tug of gravity, reducing all elevations to one uniform level, and the incessant quakes caused by the other satellites as they passed and repassed Europa in their orbits.

Carlos also observes that the music's optimistic ending is a response to Arthur C. Clarke's suggestion (in the same book) that there may be life beneath the cracked surface.

'Io' (4:28)
Carlos's musical portrait of the moon Io (another of Jupiter's satellites) returns us once again to the agitated sound world of 'Phobos And Deimos'. Here, the main influence is Baroque music, which is felt in the driving, repetitive rhythms, the contrapuntal (many stranded) manner of building up the thematic material – which gives rise to some densely layered part writing – and the *passacaglia* structure, in which the music is constantly varied over a repeating bass line. Carlos states in her notes that this approach enables her to suggest the continuously varying surface of the moon, which is known for its ceaseless volcanic activity.

'Callisto' (4:28)
Callisto (the final Jupiter moon to be referenced in the suite) has a simpler three-part (ABA) musical structure. Section A, which runs from 0:00-1:45 (and later returns at 3:19), is relatively relaxed in character and features lyrical melodic phrases which are allocated to woodwind-like timbres (oboe and clarinet). The B section (from 1:54-3:18) is dark and foreboding in its varied sounds and often fragmentary textures, and, as a result of being conceived in 5/4 time, has a much more ambiguous rhythmic feel (listen for the short repeating fragment to get your bearings). This particular moon is known for having numerous craters, including a very large one known as Valhalla, which one might perhaps relate to the metaphorical musical vacuum represented by the music's B section.

'Rhea' (1:50)
The shortest movement in the *Moonscapes* suite, 'Rhea' is the first of three portraits of the moons of Saturn. This is another satellite with a heavily cratered surface, provoking a musical response from Carlos, which is

correspondingly quite changeable. The music switches from being restful to then suddenly rhythmically agitated, as well as varied in instrumentation. From a compositional perspective, Carlos states that she is employing 'tri-tonality' in this piece, implying, in other words, that three different keys are being heard simultaneously. It is not necessary to understand the theory behind this to appreciate the aural effect of the approach, which is essentially one of harmonic instability. Related to this is Carlos's use of the 'cluster', meaning a dissonant high-pitched chord produced by overlaying several pitches at close interval range. This can be heard especially prominently in the passage from 0:00-0:32 and again at 1:34 to the end, the sound possessing an almost artificial electronic quality, in a manner reminiscent of European avant-garde composers such as Stockhausen in his early electronic studies and György Ligeti in his piece 'Atmospheres' (which was famously used in Kubrick's *2001: A Space Odyssey*).

'Titan' (3:43)
Titan, the largest of the moons of Saturn, is given a musical treatment which, in Carlos's words, is meant to suggest the 'enigma' of whether there is life below the 'hydro-carbon rich atmosphere' which obscures the surface. The result is a captivating and highly atmospheric piece, with a predominant emphasis on the 'darker' low ranges of instruments whose timbres are often suggestive of woodwind and brass. Most impressive is the opening section, whose undulating rhythms, overlaid with interjections of the cluster-type chords encountered in the previous movement, effectively suggest the planet's mysterious atmosphere, from which emerges a questioning lyrical melody played by a tuba-like instrument. Elsewhere, there are passages in this movement that remind one of Debussy, as well as Carlos's inspiration for the suite – Holst.

'Iapetus' (5:48)
The concluding portrait of the Saturn trilogy focuses on Iapetus, a moon that Carlos finds interesting on account of its strongly contrasting sides, the one black, the other bright, giving rise to a musical response that is based on two main themes. The first is of a noble character expressed via a brass-like timbre and is developed between 0:00-2:15, gradually becoming more impassioned before culminating in a dissonant climactic chord. This gives way to a contrasting section, which is characterised by a busier dance-like melody in the familiar Carlos 'Scherzo' vein. After this music has been developing for a time, it is joined (from 3:02) by interjections of the noble melody, now rhythmically re-worked to fit the new pace before entering a calmer, more static section, during which we encounter fragmentary statements of both the latter and the scherzo tune. Following this, the music begins to build again until, at 4:31, the noble theme becomes more triumphantly dominant, although it soon gives way once more to the dance-

like material. We then encounter a final section, which Carlos refers to as 'solo percussion toccata' – a sudden and surprising shift of gear at this point – before a brief orchestral crescendo signals the end of the suite.

Beauty In The Beast (1986)

Personnel:
Wendy Carlos: GDS and Synergy Synthesizers, Synton Syntovox SPX-216
Vocoder, performance, arranging, recording and production
Annemarie Franklin: 'assistance, ideas and logistics'
Record label: Audion Recording Company SYN 200/SYNCD 200
Format: LP/CD
Recorded at Carlos's Loft studio, Greenwich Village, New York
Release date: 1986
Highest chart position: did not chart
Running time: 57:46

Carlos's next album, *Beauty In The Beast*, saw her moving briefly to
Audion, a label founded by her friend, electronic artist Larry Fast, whose
pseudonym, 'Synergy', had ironically been adopted by the Digital Keyboards
company for the pioneering synthesizer instrument that Carlos employed
on *Digital Moonscapes*. Established in 1986, Audion's name refers to the
three-electrode vacuum tube invented by Lee De Forest in 1908 (an image of
which also adorns the centre label of the company's LP releases), reflecting
the company's interest in pursuing the highest technical standards in audio
recording. Musically speaking, Audion's primary focus was on contemporary
instrumental electronic music of the 'New Age' variety, making the label a
particularly appropriate setting for the musical direction that Carlos was now
taking, namely, a globally focused musical aesthetic possessing a particular
affinity with the 'world music' genre.

Beauty In The Beast is, once again, a showcase for Carlos's original
music, whose character, as with many of the albums discussed in this book,
arises from a combination of compositional exploration and technological
innovation. Specifically, Carlos is continuing to pursue her research into
the possibilities of digital sound design, not only to create new timbres but
also as a means of solving the musical problems presented by the various
global forms of music that she is attempting to evoke in her pieces. One
of the most significant innovations here is Carlos's use of a wide range of
altered tunings to capture the essence of musical languages of non-Western
cultures. In effect, she is moving her compositional style beyond the Western
'equal-tempered' tuning system in which the pitch scheme is divided into
12 equal semitones. This was a development that was made possible by the
Synergy, which allowed for detailed editing of the frequency tables of each
timbre, enabling the sounds to be re-tuned to any scale Carlos required. The
effects of this can be readily perceived across the album, quite obviously on
tracks such as 'Incantation', 'Just Imaginings' and 'Beauty In The Beast', and
in some cases, are brought into close relation with the more familiar equal-
tempered systems, as in 'Poem For Bali', which combines gamelan music with
a traditional orchestra. Three of the tracks – 'Just Imaginings', 'That's Just It'

and 'Yusae-Aisae' (pronounced 'You Say-I Say') – are notable for employing what Carlos refers to as a 'super-just' tuning system (she is obviously punning on this term in the first two titles), in which the traditional eight-note octave is divided into 144 discrete pitches, providing a means for her to experiment with a variety of new chord combinations.

The sounds developed for *Beauty In The Beast*, which, in many cases, emulate specific instruments from outside the Western instrument tradition, also represent a significant departure for Carlos. In an interview with *Downbeat* in March 1987, she commented that '*Beauty In The Beast* is, I think, the first recording to have the extrapolated type of timbres that are all based on acoustical models that no longer are limited to the LSI Philharmonic, as we call it', adding – in another interview for *Mix* magazine in the same year – that her timbres...

> ...grew out of the traditionally rich sounds of the past. I wanted to take a step in which all the sounds were different and yet based on what had come before. So, it was a learning step of making new timbres that had never been heard before.

Like *Digital Moonscapes*, *Beauty In The Beast* fared well with the critics. *Billboard*, for example, commented that Carlos 'expands the vocabulary of the electronic keyboard on this remarkable album ... a groundbreaking performance'. Andrea Houtkin, writing in the authoritative *Computer Music Journal* in Summer 1988, concluded her review with the following remarks:

> One hopes that listeners do not allow their imaginations to run so free as to only be able to describe these collective selections on this album as a 'soundtrack to a dream, just ready to be experienced', but rather, as an offering of arduous research, study and experimentation and beauty itself.

'Incantation' (6:47)

This striking ritualistic piece is intended to suggest an imagined ceremony in a Tibetan or Bhutanese monastery and features a tuning which Carlos gleaned from listening to recordings of Tibetan ritual music. Authentic timbres are also devised using digital synthesis techniques, including Tibetan bells, horns and abrasive-sounding reed instruments. Much of the music is drone-like in character, consisting of layered, sustained notes which harmonise to produce dissonant chords, creating a mood of tension and anticipation. Carlos also makes use of digital reverb to situate the music in a large sounding space and, at certain points, employs dynamic movement of sounds within the stereo field (see the track's beginning, for example). In certain parts of the piece – 1.48-2.30, 3.05-3.49 and later at 4.21 (as an accompaniment to bell-like sounds) – we hear a deeply pitched vocal-like drone, which, according to Carlos, was generated using her Synton vocoder.

'Beauty In The Beast' (3:57)

This is a fascinating piece which occupies a sound world all of its own. Carlos notes that she used two specially designed tunings for this piece, entitled 'alpha' and 'beta'. Constructing these scales involves dividing the octave by various means into a larger number of individual pitch 'segments', the effect being to create a more subtly refined palette of notes to choose from, which initially sound mis-tuned to the un-adjusted ear. As Carlos has observed of the alpha scale, 'hearing it for the first time is like eating sushi for the first time. It's exotic'. The piece has an unpredictable form and makes use of irregular time signatures, although it is unified by a distinctive lyrical, melodic idea which reappears at certain junctures. Metallic percussion sounds are also a prominent feature of the track, often being employed to create a repetitive textural backdrop. Especially impressive is the darkly seductive middle section between 1.27-2.35, which builds to a carousel-like effect at 2.00. One is reminded at times of the metallic sounds (e.g. at 2:18) of David Bowie's 'Weeping Wall' (on the album *Low*), co-produced with Brian Eno, who, incidentally, was also undertaking similar experiments with non-Western music in the 1980s.

'Poem For Bali' (17:40)

'Poem For Bali', the longest track on the album, is one of Carlos's most substantial compositions to date and is conceived on a scale not encountered since her earlier *Sonic Seasonings* album. Like the latter, it also offers an immersive listening experience, in this case, an Indonesian-themed sonic tour of the musical culture of the island of Bali (which Carlos had visited in 1983) through an evocation of the unique sounds of the gamelan ensemble. Indeed, it was the experience of Indonesian music that was the main catalyst in Carlos's decision to create *Beauty In The Beast* in the first place (its importance to Carlos's conception is also indicated by the album cover, which reproduces an image of the Balinese Ubud style of painting by W.Y. Weca).

To convincingly convey the sounds of Balinese music, Carlos has accurately synthesized the various gongs and metallophones of the gamelan ensemble and has made use of the standard Indonesian tunings of the slendro and pelog scales. Put simply, the slendro is a five-note scale tuned at approximately equidistant intervals, while the pelog has seven notes like the traditional Western major scale. However, the interval distances (gaps between the notes) vary considerably in size from a semitone to a minor third. Carlos comments, however, that in realising the music, she had to make adjustments to these scale tunings as a compromise to make them fit with the more traditional orchestral music that appears at certain junctures in the piece (e.g. section 9). In performance, Carlos has also attempted to emulate the performance style of the gamelan, particularly the characteristic speeding up and slowing down of the music. The piece has a complex rondo-type structure (meaning that certain key elements return periodically), comprising ten main sections, roughly laid out as follows:

Part 1: a mysterious introduction (suggesting dawn on the Isle of Bali, perhaps). A short melodic phrase is repeated on a flute-like instrument (presumably an emulation of the Indonesian end-blown *suling*) over a complex textured backdrop, which gradually builds in intensity.

Part 2: more rhythmic activity with delay affected metallic sounding timbres, convincingly evoking the metallophones of the gamelan, whose repeating patterns are overlaid to create a complex texture.

Part 3: the *suling* theme heard during Part 1 returns over a gentle, sustained backdrop and a shimmering metallic texture.

Part 4: the section referred to by Carlos as the 'Barong dance'. This is where we hear an authentic emulation of a gamelan performance, characterised by interlocking patterns played at various speeds. This is essentially the dramatic centrepiece of the track, demonstrating Carlos's strong affinity with the style.

Part 5: a calmer, more meditative section, during which there are further reminiscences of the earlier *suling* music. This music becomes darker in mood, the *suling* music continuing with interjections of the shimmering metallic arabesques heard in Part 3. Next, a more gentle section emerges, now with a regular pulse, featuring the metallophone instruments playing slower repeating patterns. Soon, we move into a wind-swept terrain as the gentle undulating pattern slows to a standstill.

Part 7: a more optimistic mood ensues and we are once again greeted by the sounds of the barong dance, elements of which now occur in a more fragmentary manner.

Part 8: in keeping with the rondo structure, the *suling* music returns once again, which is now conflated with the more repetitive metallophone music.

Part 9: what Carlos has described as a 'mini-concerto' for the gamelan ensemble and the orchestra, climaxing at 15:00.

Part 10: the piece concludes with the evocative *suling* music, which is heard over sustained textures with a choral character conflated with the rhythmic metallophone textures.

'Just Imaginings' (12:07)

Another of the LP's more extended and elaborate compositions, 'Just Imaginings' is the first of three tracks to employ what Carlos refers to as her 'super-just' of 'harmonic' tuning system, whose disconcerting effect is apparent from the outset, although the ear soon adjusts to the difference. Musically, the piece is an interesting fusion of repetitive electronic textures and more traditional melodic material, heard in relation to chord structures that would sound conventional were they not frequently overlaid with dissonance. The repetitive introductory music brings to mind earlier electronic composers such as Raymond Scott, while the more abstract electronic textures we encounter (such as in the section between 3:54-5:15) are reminiscent of Carlos's earlier experimental 'Timesteps' style on *A Clockwork Orange*. The structure, on the whole, feels free-form, with juxtapositions of material that are often stylistically incongruous with one another, the various sections appearing to emerge for a time and then subsequently disappearing from focus. It may aid the listener to keep in mind that key points of transition (when we encounter markedly different musical material and textures) occur at approximately 0:51, 2:17, 3:54, 5:36, 7:03, 7:48, 8:35, 9:00, 9:33, 11.04-end.

'That's Just It' (3:36)
One of the more immediately accessible pieces on the album, 'That's Just It' has an affinity with the 1950s 'cool jazz' style associated with artists such as Miles Davis. A prominent focus is on the sounds of the jazzy brass/wind ensemble, with trumpet and saxophone timbres providing a solo contribution. Like a number of the pieces on the album, the music is built on an unchanging harmonic base, which supports instrumental lines with an improvised character. Once again, Carlos is employing 'super-just' intonation in the composition of the piece, which appears less noticeable (if we have listened to the album tracks in sequence, then our ears will, of course, have already become well adjusted).

'Yusae-Aisae' (3:12)
This track, which showcases Carlos's third experiment with 'super-just' tuning, contains elements suggestive of both Middle Eastern and Indian music. It features a repetitive solo melody (employing an 'Arabic' scale type) performed using a synthesizer patch constructed from the combined timbres of a horn and xylophone. Accompanying this is a droning chord reminiscent of a harmonium (an organ-like instrument commonly found in Indian music). After half a minute, a drum part is introduced, which evokes the sound of a *tabla* and this plays a repeating pattern in the irregular time signature of 5/4, eventually joined by interjecting phrases on trumpets. The music is gradually thickened through the addition of new instruments until the droning backdrop appears to be on the brink of overwhelming the group.

'C'est Afrique' (6:13)
Like 'Poem For Bali', the 'C'est Afrique' was inspired by Carlos's direct experiences of the musical cultures in question; in this case, the result of several visits to the African continent. The 1980s was, of course, a period in which a number of musical artists took an interest in the music of Africa, most notably Paul Simon for his *Graceland* album, released in the same year as *Beauty In The Beast*. Western artists were particularly inspired by

the complex rhythmic content of African music, as is the case with Carlos, who has used digital synthesis techniques to devise an African percussion ensemble, which includes authentic drum tunings. At certain points, the piece also features a distinctive repeating vocal chant element, which was again created using a vocoder. 'C'est Afrique' has four contrasting sections, running respectively from 0:00-1:44, 1:44-2:50, 2:50-4:48 and 4:48-end, which, as in 'Just Imaginings', simply segue from one to the next. In this sense, the piece comes across as a series of individual portraits of Africa rather than as a unified composition, although some material does recur at certain points.

'A Woman's Song' (4:09)
According to Carlos's liner notes, the album's final track, 'A Woman's Song', draws upon a rustic melody sung by a Bulgarian Shepherdess. In its sonic realisation, however, Carlos is again drawing upon an Indian music influence, incorporating sounds of a *tambura* (a four-string, long-necked lute) and a *dilruba* (a bowed instrument). The track also incorporates noticeable electronic effects, including a digital delay, which is used to produce the rhythmic movement of the percussion hits heard at the outset. Musically, the track is simple in conception, being largely comprised of a chord drone of the interval of a fifth (one of the barest sounding chord structures), over which are heard phrases of a melody performed in an improvised manner (suggestive of an Indian raga).

Peter And The Wolf/Carnival Of The Animals – Part II (1988)

Personnel:
Wendy Carlos: synthesis, sampling, arranging, recording and production
LSI Philharmonic: digital orchestra, credited as performer
Al Yankovic: poems and spoken narration
Annemarie Franklin: 'associate production'
Record label: CBS Masterworks FM 44567/MK 44567
Format: LP/CD
Recorded at Carlos's Loft studio, Greenwich Village, New York
Release date: October 1988
Highest chart position: US: 8 (*Billboard* Top Crossover Albums)
Running time: 57:57

Carlos's next musical endeavour was an unexpected one, to say the least – a collaboration with American comedian and musician 'Weird Al' Yankovic on an imaginative update of two perennial classics of children's music: *Peter And The Wolf* and *Carnival Of The Animals*. This unlikely meeting of minds occurred as a result of a suggestion by CBS Masterworks, who envisaged an album release for the 1988 Christmas market (coinciding as it happens with the 20th anniversary of the release of *Switched-On Bach*). Yankovic was, by the time of his collaboration with Carlos, a household name due to his parodies of contemporary popular music, most famously the single 'Eat It' (a send-up of Michael Jackson's 'Beat It'), which charted in both the US and the UK, and the Madonna re-working, 'Like A Surgeon'. This comic style is similarly applied to *Peter And The Wolf*, whose narrative Yankovic embellishes with knowing and often darkly humorous asides. With *Carnival Of The Animals*, however, Yankovic contributed a brand-new script inspired by the original Ogden Nash poems, which neatly complemented Carlos's imaginatively composed music.

In contrast to the technological resources that had been available for her last classical project, *Switched-On Brandenburgs*, Carlos was now employing tools and techniques that were light years ahead of the analogue world she had left behind following the completion of *Tron*. In both realisations, the increasingly refined digital colours of the LSI Philharmonic (which, at this stage, is being credited on the album cover as if it were a real orchestra) remain central to Carlos's orchestral conception. However, in addition to her two Synergy synthesizers, she also added several new sound design tools to her armoury, including a Kurzweil 150 digital additive synthesizer, a Yamaha RX5 drum machine and Kurzweil HX and SX 1000 Sample Modules. The ready-made, pre-recorded and synthesized sounds provided by these devices presented new colouristic possibilities for Carlos's fundamental synthesis approach, marking her first attempts at incorporating and blending sampled instrument sounds into her orchestrations. In reference to this departure, Carlos commented in an interview for *Keyboard* magazine in January 1989 that samples 'proved to be very helpful in sweetening the strings and heavy brass I'd already generated – the mix of the two was better than either was alone. A lot of people are doing that more and more'. Carlos was also now working on Apple Macintosh Plus/Levco Prodigy computers, running a music sequencing software package called 'Performer' (by Mark of the Unicorn), which afforded a much greater level of control over the recording process. In addition, she was benefitting from the recently developed MIDI (Music Instrument Digital Interface) protocol, which enabled more efficient synchronisation of hardware and software (although this was not without its problems). She was thus increasingly embracing the digital electronic music aesthetic of the period, retaining her reputation as an artist willing to work at the cutting edge of technological innovation.

While it is fair to say that the album passed relatively unnoticed by the critics, it nonetheless has the distinction of being nominated in the category of 'Best Children's Album' for the 1989 Grammy Awards. The album also marked a return to form for Carlos in the charts, reaching the number eight spot in the *Billboard* Top Crossover Albums rankings.

Peter And The Wolf (Sergei Prokofiev)
Sergei Prokofiev's *Peter And The Wolf* Op. 67 (composed in 1936) first became widely known to audiences through the 1959 Grammy Award-winning recording narrated by Peter Ustinov and accompanied by the Philharmonia Orchestra conducted by Herbert Von Karajan. Several alternative accounts have been recorded since then, although none have been given a maverick re-imagining of the pairing of Carlos-Yankovic, which updates both text and music in ways that certainly had not been envisaged by Prokofiev!

Introduction (3:58)
The original *Peter And The Wolf* score is prefixed by an introduction, in which the different musical themes and instruments associated with the main characters of the drama – the bird, duck, cat, grandfather, Peter and the rifle shots of the hunters – are briefly performed so that they can later be identified. In the new version, these are given a comic twist by Yankovic's script, the animals now receiving absurd names – bird (Billy), duck (Bruce), cat (Louis) – and the grandfather momentarily confused with the Godfather (Don Ameche). Yankovic also nearly forgets to mention the wolf and introduces a new character, 'Bob the Janitor', instead of Peter, with Prokofiev's famous theme for the latter now being amusingly substituted with a snippet of whacky accordion music performed by Yankovic himself. With the exception of this (and a brief quotation of 'We are Siamese' in reference to the cat), the thematic music otherwise remains intact and in its original orchestration, which has, of course, been digitally emulated.

Peter And The Wolf (27:52)

Carlos's realisation of *Peter And The Wolf* signals a return to her classical music arranging roots in a version which mostly adheres to Prokofiev's original score, with the composer's orchestrations now being emulated using her painstakingly constructed LSI Philharmonic sound library. It is certainly among the most advanced of her classical realisations to date, primarily due to the complexity of Prokofiev's orchestral writing, in which individual instruments are given distinctive musical lines which are challenging to render realistically in performance. The flute part, for example, which represents the bird, is highly ornate and rhythmically intricate, requiring a realisation that is necessarily sensitive to a flautist's idiosyncratic approach to phrasing. Carlos's authentic rendering of this and other instrumental traits throughout the piece is a testament both to her knowledge of the orchestra and her own performance skills. While the instrument sounds themselves possess an artificial character relative to their acoustic equivalents, they are nonetheless colourful and vibrant and, taken together, present a wholly convincing digital orchestral aesthetic. Carlos's emulations are arguably at their most successful when dealing with the strings, winds (flute, clarinet, oboe and bassoon) and brass instruments (the three horns used to characterise the wolf) and at their weakest when imitating percussion, particularly drums, whose sounds (especially when repeated in close proximity) are not as subtly rendered.

Although she mostly observes Prokofiev's musical score to the letter, on occasion, Carlos cannot resist introducing brief quotations from other famous pieces, reminding us of her cleverly constructed collage of themes in 'Pompous Circumstances' (on the album *By Request*). The first of these interjections, which is obviously done for comedy value, occurs at the culmination of the scene in which the wolf catches the duck and swallows him whole (8:26-10:35). We hear an extended segment of the iconic high-pitched string music which accompanies the knife murder scene in the Hitchcock film *Psycho* (composed by Bernard Hermann). A second example occurs at 17:02 during the sequence in which the bird teases the wolf. Carlos references the famous chugging string chords of the 'Dances Of The Young Girls' music from Stravinsky's *The Rite Of Spring* (a theme likely to be familiar to most listeners from its use in Disney's *Fantasia*). Carlos also briefly quotes the piercing *Psycho* music again in this section for good measure. Other moments of musical comedy include the synthesizer-produced duck quacks and miaows, a brief snippet of Bach's Two Part Invention No. 8 (10:58) interpolated into the cat's theme, the accordion music of Bob the Janitor, which is inexplicably re-introduced at 14:10, and the French can-can, which is worked into the bird music at 16:39. Carlos also provides a comic sound design touch to underpin the appearance of the hunters (between 19:26-20:56), who are amusingly characterised by Yankovic as members of the National Rifle Association and now carry 'magnums, uzis and bazookas'.

To overstate the new scale of their weaponry, Carlos employs a series of explosion sound effects, which, needless to say, somewhat overshadow Prokofiev's original score, where rifle shots are simply imitated using timpani.

The Carnival Of The Animals – Part II (Carlos/Camille Saint-Saens)
Carnival Of The Animals – Part II is a collection of original pieces intended as a sequel to the famous suite of orchestral animal characterisations by French composer Camille Saint-Saens (1835-1921). The original work contains many imaginative and evocative pieces, some of which have become widely known to audiences, including the 'The Swan' and 'Aquarium'. In addition to drawing upon Saint-Saens' original music at certain points, Carlos once again employs a number of 'knowing' musical quotations which compliment Yankovic's often hilarious script.

'Introduction' (1:20)
Yankovic offers a brief spoken introduction to the work, which is followed by a short piece based on Saint-Saens' own introductory music, with its characteristic shimmering piano textures. There is a unique twist, however, in that we hear Saint-Saens' simple theme (on strings) inverted – in other words, the melody has been turned upside down. This is a technique commonly employed by modern composers to obtain more mileage from their material and listeners who know the original piece will still recognise its relationship to Carlos's re-working in spite of the unorthodox treatment.

'Aardvark' (1:47)
To announce the entry of the Aardvark, the music begins with a dramatic brass-led fanfare before concluding on an anticipatory chord. For her characterisation of the animal, Carlos uses a winding chromatic scale played slowly, sounding like a lazy version of 'Flight Of The Bumblebee'. This lead line is played by two instruments, firstly a synthesised horn and then a tuba, accompanied by delicate strings and percussion flourishes.

'Hummingbirds' (0:58)
In this piece, Carlos draws heavily upon Saint-Saens' piece 'The Swan' – here played by a solo piccolo befitting the small, lightweight character of the Hummingbird – and sets the music in a scherzo-like rhythmic framing. Carlos also peppers the music with high-pitched, rapid tremolo figures to suggest the beating of a Hummingbird's wings.

'Snails' (2:03)
To depict the Snails, Carlos uses what she refers to as a 'lugubrious' rhythmic effect, combining three separate instrumental lines, each with their own individual timings. Underlying the music is a pulse of four, gently performed on the piano as an arpeggio figure, against which we can hear a brass-like

instrument playing triplets (that is, rhythms grouped in threes). A few moments later, a wind instrument enters, playing a melody in two beat groupings, which just happens to be the theme from Rossini's William Tell Overture, hence our first classical music quotation and yet another reference to a piece that has obsessed Carlos since *A Clockwork Orange*.

'Alligator' (1:15)
This short piece has a swung jazzy feel and employs quirky, repetitive melodic ideas designed to suggest the 'hip' character of the Alligator. The xylophone is the dominant instrument here, which has been chosen by Carlos to highlight the creature's sharp teeth.

'Amoeba' (1:52)
We now have a melancholy musical setting in waltz time whose purpose is to suggest the pitifully small size of the Amoeba. The music has a graceful character and is beautifully orchestrated, combining a delicate flute melody with sustained strings and a celesta-like pattern which runs throughout.

'Pigeons' (1:56)
The music of 'Pigeons' is a combination of two elements – an urgent, pulsing motif on brass instruments (reminding one of Carlos's music for *Tron*) and a more graceful flute melody set in a waltz style, peppered with percussion flourishes. The first element appears intended to suggest the aggressive nature of the birds, who 'terrorise folks with their constant dive-bombing', the latter the more graceful aspect of their flight, the percussion interjections suggesting their tendency to off-load on the unsuspecting pedestrian.

'Shark' (2:17)
For the music of the Shark, Carlos introduces another reference to the Saint-Saens original, this time employing the familiar watery-sounding passages from 'Aquarium', which are highly apt to suggest the habitat of the creature in question. The threatening nature of the shark itself is depicted with another classic Carlos signature motif – the melody of the 'Dies Irae', previously familiar to listeners through her two film soundtracks *A Clockwork Orange* and *The Shining*. Carlos also manages to work in a more recent popular culture reference to John Williams' famous two-note theme for the film *Jaws*. In its seamless melding of familiar musical elements, this is undoubtedly one of the standout musical constructions of the suite.

'Cockroaches' (1:40)
The Cockroaches are depicted through an interplay of two main themes. The first is a nervous-sounding arpeggio figure in the lower strings, which suggests the cockroaches' fear of being crunched underfoot (as per Yankovic's introductory poem). The second is a scurrying figure played by

winds, piano and percussion, which suggests the insects fleeing when the kitchen light is switched on.

'Iguana' (0:35)
This brief piece, which amounts to a few short phrases, has a regal quality suggested by the stately string and brass chords, suggesting an influence of early courtly music perhaps.

'Vulture' (3:14)
The longest piece in the suite, 'Vulture' begins with a dramatic introduction suggesting the grim circumstances of the scavenger's existence, which, as Yankovic's dark poem describes, is mainly concerned with waiting patiently until another creature 'croaks' and then feasting upon its corpse. The bulk of the piece is a slow clarinet/saxophone-led blues number, which lends the subject a certain 'coolness' of character that may perhaps have been influenced by Disney's depiction of these birds in *The Jungle Book*. Carlos's use of occasional ominous tolling clock chimes during this section, implying that 'the hour is nigh' for the Vulture's next victim, is a darkly humorous musical touch.

'Unicorn' (1:25)
The music depicting the Unicorn – amusingly referred to by Carlos as 'stallion-esque' – has a certain majesty conveyed by the combination of brass (specifically the horn, a nice play on the Unicorn's most distinctive feature) and timpani. It is possible that Carlos was influenced by the famous melody for the 1970s TV show *Black Beauty*, probably the most internationally well-known equine-themed music prior to this time. Elsewhere, the music has an archaic, almost Medieval character (see 0:34-0:55), evoking a distant imagined past for this fantasy creature that Yankovic suggests is 'just a myth, which is to say they don't exist'.

'Poodle' (2:51)
Perhaps the most ludicrous creature to appear in the suite, the Poodle is given a complex musical characterisation as a means of suggesting the dog's confusion as to its identity. In particular, Carlos uses this as an opportunity to revisit a number of earlier themes. The music begins with a waltz for accordion and percussion (which feels like a possible reference to Patti Page's 'How much is that doggie in the window?'), followed by a section of the William Tell Overture theme associated with the 'Snails' (again in a polyrhythmic setting). We then have a brief reminiscence of the music of 'The Swan' (used in 'Hummingbirds') on piccolo, followed by more waltz material, and then the Vulture's bluesy theme returns on clarinet. The final section reprises the scurrying music associated with the Cockroaches and there is also a brief hint of the Shark.

'Finale' (2:53)

The dramatic finale, which is in a more complex multi-sectioned form, provides a fittingly triumphant conclusion to the proceedings. Carlos describes the piece as having three 'parade' themes and a carnival coda, whose main sections appear at the following points:

0:00: Prelude – reprising the earlier introductory piano/string section and concluding with another brief snippet of Bach's Two-Part Invention In F.

0:47: First theme (trumpet tone) – heard twice, with added orchestration on second occasion and piano lead.

1:19: Second theme – a more urgent, rhythmically insistent section, characterised by call and answer between different instrumental sections.

1:47: Third theme on strings – in a lyrical, romantic vein, joined by brass.

2:02: The first theme recapitulated.

2:32: Carnival coda – the music crescendos to its grand finale.

Switched-On Bach 2000 (1992)

Personnel:
Wendy Carlos: synthesis, sequencing, performance, arranging, recording and production
Record label: Telarc CD-80323
Format: CD
Recorded at Carlos's Loft studio, Greenwich Village, New York
Release date: 1992
Highest chart position: US: 6 (*Billboard* Top Classical Albums)
Running time: 53:50

Carlos's next release, *Switched-On Bach 2000*, was a project to revisit and update her original *Switched-On Bach* recording in the light of more than two decades of considerable technological change, as well as artistic maturation over the course of nine studio albums and three film soundtracks. As such, we appear to have come full circle in the electronic odyssey begun by Carlos in 1968, with a recording that is both nostalgic and forward-looking and which, at the same time, gives cause for reflection on her many achievements. It should be added, incidentally, that the album was not issued to coincide with the millennium itself but rather eight years prior to mark the 25th anniversary of the original *Switched-On Bach* release.

Re-recording past repertoire was not, of course, uncommon in the classical field, where it is expected that an artist will revisit and update their performance practice as their concept of a particular musical work changes. Pianist Glenn Gould, for example (an avowed fan of Carlos's early classical projects), famously revisited his acclaimed 1955 recording of Bach's *The Goldberg Variations* in 1981, bringing new perspectives to his earlier interpretation and thereby shedding new light on the work as a whole.

Certainly, reviewing the repertoire to re-think earlier interpretations had a part to play in Carlos's decision to re-make *Switched-On Bach*, especially as regards her desire to finally resolve the problem of the second movement of Brandenburg Concerto No. 3, which she had already grappled with for the second time on *Switched-On Brandenburgs*. The album also afforded her the possibility of finally realising her ambition to produce a synthesizer arrangement of Bach's substantial Toccata & Fugue In D Minor, which is the album's main bonus track. However, Carlos also had objectives for her new Bach recordings which related to practical possibilities that she could not have entertained for the 1968 album. Foremost among these was her desire to apply the experiments with altered tunings that she had begun on *Beauty In The Beast* in the context of Baroque music, in particular 'meantone' tuning. In an interview for *Keyboard* magazine in August 1992, Carlos explained why she had chosen to apply alternative tunings to Bach:

Because it sounds good! It's like, why use spices and seasonings when cooking? Because it tastes good. You don't need any more justification. But the improvement is subtle. If you point it out to people, most will hear the difference and prefer the better way. That's what this album is about. This is the better way, the way that Bach himself did it. Bach *never* liked equal temperament.

Carlos then proceeded to discuss the inaccurate mythology that had built up around Bach's preferences for equal-tempered tuning, explaining how 'meantone' and 'cyclic' tuning better reflected Bach's tastes for pitch discrepancies.

Digital synthesizers remain at the heart of Carlos's sound design operation on *Switched on Bach 2000*, by now the range of tools having been significantly expanded to include not only her two trusty Synergy synths but also three Mulogix Slave 32s, Yamaha's TX 802 and SY77 synthesizers, two Kurzweil FS 150s and four Kurzweil 1000s. According to Carlos's liner notes, the Moog synthesizer, which had been the mainstay of the original *Switched-On Bach*, also features on one solitary occasion on the album, although she does not specify which track, thus challenging the listener to spot it. In the later stages of the project, Carlos also took advantage of newly emerging Digital Audio Workstation technology, adopting Digidesign's relatively recently released Pro Tools software. This allowed for highly refined editing of MIDI-recorded parts, including precise alterations of timing and loudness of individual pitches. The precision and cleanliness of the sound of the final recording can certainly be regarded as a by-product of working with such software, which has since become an industry standard. Given these high-tech facilities, it is perhaps surprising to observe that, compared to the original recording of *Switched-On Bach*, the updated version still took more than twice as long to complete (around ten months). This contradicts any notion that the mainly digital tools involved in the process were necessarily making things easier, Carlos recalling having to deal with frequent bugs and system issues. In realising Bach's music, Carlos often pays tribute to the first album by reintroducing timbres associated with the original interpretations (including the novel white noise effect), which, in their new digital guise, often impart a much greater level of realism (see 'Air On A G String' and Prelude No. 7, for example). Carlos also revives her hocketing technique in several tracks – which she had, of course, not yet developed at the time of completing the original *Switched-On Bach* – and employs a similarly imaginative approach to the use of spatial effects (here being generated by such tools as the AMS 15-80S and Lexicon PCM-42 digital delay units).

Appropriately, perhaps, given the level of technical expertise involved in its production, *Switched-On Bach 2000* was issued on Telarc, a record label recognised for its audiophile pedigree. Carlos also fared much better this time with the album's artwork, which presented a more respectful image of Bach sitting at a harpsichord, now transformed into a computer workstation, complete with monitor and QWERTY keyboards.

Happy 25th, S-OB (0:40)

To wish her album a happy 25th anniversary, Carlos opens with a short, specially composed piece in the Bach style, its musical content anticipating the Sinfonia To Cantata No. 29, which follows. Carlos has stated that this track is mixed around 3dB lower than the following Sinfonia to give the latter more impact.

Sinfonia To Cantata No. 29 (3:35)

Carlos's re-working of the Sinfonia has a bold 'in your face' character which makes the original version sound rather polite in comparison. The metallic (almost gamelan-like) timbres that Carlos has chosen for the main theme, which takes the form of a continuous stream of 16th-note scales and arpeggio figures, imparts an almost mechanical quality suggestive of an 18th-century musical automaton. Carlos's trademark hocketing technique is also once again in play, creating a sense of antiphonal interaction between phrases and imparting a vibrant three-dimensionality to the music that is absent from the relatively static 1968 recording. The accompanying orchestral chords are dominated by an impressively authentic-sounding Baroque trumpet timbre, which Carlos created using her Synergy.

'Air On A G String' (3:15)

Carlos's re-imagining of this perennial Bach favourite (taken from the Orchestral Suite No. 3 In D major (BWV 1068)) is around 45 seconds longer than the 1968 version and, overall, comes across as a more relaxed and contemplative affair. While the re-interpretation appears to lack a certain analogue warmth in its new digital guise (for example, the schmaltzy sentimentality of the vibrato has been significantly tamed in this version), there is a pleasing clarity to the overall mix and the instrumental sounds are generally very convincing (Carlos has again chosen to emulate a woodwind group). A key factor which contributes to the realism of this recording is Carlos's decision to place the ensemble in a simulated reverberant environment and organise the individual sounds in the stereo field in a way that a listener would recognise from a live concert setting.

Two-Part Invention In F Major (0:47)

For the popular Two-Part Invention No. 8 In F Major, Carlos has employed a distinctly metallic timbre, which serves to further bring out the machine-like qualities of the broken chord patterning on which the piece is based. Her hocketing style, which, it will be recalled, was a common arranging strategy (from *The Well-Tempered Synthesizer* onwards) when dealing with simple textured pieces of this nature, is also a key part of the presentation. The music, which is rendered at lightning speed (but, nonetheless, slower than her first version), appears to ricochet around the stereo field and is accompanied by constant shifts of timbre.

Two-Part Invention In B-Flat Major (1:23)
In the Two-Part Invention No. 14 In B-Flat, the hocketing effect is again in evidence, with Carlos now assigning the fragmented phrases of the music to what she refers to as 'imaginary solo instruments' placed around the stereo picture. The sounds employed here reflect, according to Carlos's liner notes, her favourite Moog patches (in other words, tone colour settings), some of which recall those employed in her original realisation of this piece.

Two-Part Invention In D Minor (0:59)
Carlos's timbral setting of Invention No. 4 replaces the squelchy tones of her first version with a wider variety of fluctuating timbres (again, harpsichord-like metallic qualities are key to the sound), enhanced, as in the original version, using spatial effects to vary the acoustic perspective.

'Jesu, Joy Of Man's Desiring' (3:33)
At over half a minute longer, this updated realisation of one of Carlos's favourite Bach melodies comes across, in one sense, as a tribute to the original, mainly due to her use of a white noise waveform for the counter-melody (see 0:23-0:47, for example), although this is more deeply buried in the mix. The continuously flowing main tune has a more stilted and regimented character compared to the first version, however, perhaps as a result of the sequencing process, which is further emphasised by the metallic timbre. This is counterbalanced by the more warmly synthesized surrounding harmonies, whose timbres include a subtle choral tone, which imparts a fullness to the mix that is absent from the relatively sparse 1968 realisation.

Prelude (5:42) And Fugue (1:48) No. 7 In E-Flat Major From Book 1 Of The Well-Tempered Clavier
In her new version of Prelude No. 7, Carlos once again employs a brass-like timbral palette, but this time, the effect is smoother and more sustained, reflecting a greatly enhanced capacity for expressively shaping the instrumental tone in real time (Carlos states that she achieved this by putting the sounds through her Synton Vocoder, using the Yamaha SY77 synthesizer to control the brightness). Overall, this is an impressive and highly realistic rendition which contrasts strongly with the original setting. In the much briefer Fugue, Carlos distinguishes the various lines using contrasting bright and muted tone colours (including elements of white noise) placed at extremes of the stereo picture.

Prelude (1:32) And Fugue (1:32) No. 2 In C Minor From Book 1 Of The Well-Tempered Clavier

Carlos's first realisation of Prelude and Fugue No. 2 on *Switched-On Bach* was already in experimental territory with its fuzzy, noise-like timbre. The new version is, in comparison, 'off-the-charts', the music now being clothed in the sounds of the gamelan ensemble she had employed on *Beauty In The Beast*. While the effect is certainly unexpected, it nonetheless perfectly suits the design of Bach's music with its rapidly executed repetitive interlocking patterns. Carlos also employs metallic colours for the Fugue, including an ambiguously tuned bass timbre, imparting a rather music-box-like character to the piece overall. This is, by far, the most unorthodox reading of Bach that Carlos has undertaken, with the exception of her 1968 experimental re-imagining of Brandenburg Concerto No. 3 Second Movement.

'Wachet Auf' (From Cantata No. 140) (4:44)

Carlos's second version of this popular Chorale Prelude is more than a minute longer and performed in a straightforwardly pedestrian manner. Its arrangement is again rather conventional in character (anything too flamboyant would upset the delicate balance of the part writing), Carlos allocating distinctive and contrasting timbres for each of the three individual lines, with only the occasional chime-like clangs serving to punctuate the hymn tune melody each time it reappears. As before, the piece serves to provide a moment of quiet contemplation before the grand finale.

Brandenburg Concerto No. 3 In G Major – First Movement (6:49)

Carlos's new (slightly slower) realisation of the First Movement of the Concerto has a markedly different sonic character to the original, her new digital sound design tools now imparting a thicker, weightier character to the music. The listener's interest is continuously refreshed by Carlos's subtle (and not-so-subtle) variation of instrumental tone colours, which causes certain details to be brought out in ways not heard previously. Often, these variations occur on a phrase-by-phrase basis, such as the delightful passage of music between 5:15 and 5:34, which coincides with the same point in the piece that was highlighted in the earlier discussion of *Switched-On Bach* (a side-by-side comparison is certainly worth undertaking to appreciate the differences).

Brandenburg Concerto No. 3 In G Major – Second Movement (2:36)

As previously discussed, Carlos had already revisited the Second Movement of Brandenburg Concerto No. 3 for her 1980 release *Switched-On Brandenburgs* in order to update the quirky experimental approach she had taken on *Switched-On Bach*. By 1992, however, she had begun to regard the second version as equally outmoded, as she remarked to *Keyboard* magazine in August of that year:

I was never totally satisfied with either of the second movements I did for the Brandenburg Three. I know that on the first record, it's fun and kaleidoscopic, but it clashes with the other movements. It's like a technicolour mole on a sepia-toned nose. And the version I did for the complete Brandenburgs was too reactionary; it went too far back the other way. I thought I could come up with a better one.

The resulting third realisation is a slow, stately piece based on a simple (flute-led) theme which came to her some years prior to her work on *Switched-On Bach 2000*. It is similar in length to her first attempt and, in a different way, is also stylistically at odds with the musical language of the Concerto. In other words, it does not feel strictly 'Baroque'; rather, it is an obviously modern pastiche in a more lightweight sentimental romantic vein, which captures something of the character of Bach in its phrasing and ornamentation but is, overall, a Carlos piece.

Brandenburg Concerto No. 3 In G Major – Third Movement (5:48)
According to the CD liner notes, Carlos was 'intimidated' by the prospect of re-working the Third Movement of the Concerto because it represented the peak of her accomplishment on the *Switched-On Bach* album. The revised version does not disappoint, however, with Carlos adopting a more relaxed pace than the original and demonstrating just as much imagination in her sound design approach, extracting many different tone colours from her digital synthesizers. She also adopts a similar strategy to the original here in the way that she has employed the stereo field to bring out the sectional part writing and applied subtle digital reverb to situate the instruments in space. Between 2:43-3:33, Carlos again uses a prominently mixed white noise timbre in the instrumental line as a homage to the Moog-saturated sound world of *Switched-On Bach*.

Toccata & Fugue In D Minor (9:01)
The album's final (bonus) track is an epic synthesizer orchestration of Bach's monumental and expansive organ work, the Toccata & Fugue In D Minor (BWV 565), a substantial undertaking for Carlos which presented a considerable challenge to her technical abilities, just as the Brandenburg Concerto No. 3 had done in 1968. Bach's Toccata & Fugue is undoubtedly one of the composer's most familiar and iconic pieces and has appeared in several orchestral arrangements by conductor luminaries such as Leopold Stokowski, Henry Wood and Eugene Ormandy. Carlos's particular inspiration appears to have been the 1927 version by Stokowski (best known through its use in the 1940 Disney film *Fantasia*), a forward-thinking musician who had experimented with the possibilities of recording technology earlier in the century. In a September 1992 interview for *Keyboard*, Carlos describes her arrangement of the Toccata & Fugue as the

'timbral tour de force attempt of the album', in which she brought together a number of tone colours in combination:

> There are places where you hear things that sound like real woodwinds, real percussion, real piano, real mallet instruments and real violin. There are lots of quotes from pipe organ sounds, which you would want in a piece like this, and some slightly Stokowski-like things reminiscent of Fantasia. It's a chop suey kind of stew, but what can I say? I like it.

Carlos's remarks here relate to the fact that, like Bach's other keyboard pieces, such as the Two-Part Inventions, the music of the Toccata & Fugue is of a relatively simple nature, often consisting of no more than two or three lines at once. As such, any realisation requires an imaginative use of instrumentation to keep the music fresh for the listener, a problem that is solved on the organ by using different instrument stops, but which, in Carlos's case, required her to draw upon the entire sonic gamut of her synthesizer armoury, as well as her innovative spatial production techniques. It is interesting to note that Carlos had already attempted to realise the Toccata & Fugue during the 1970s but had abandoned the project due to technological constraints. With the advent of MIDI and computer-based sequencing in the 1980s, however, it had now become possible to achieve the level of technical control required to bring off her interpretation, particularly as regards the coordination of timbre changes and the prevalent hocketing aspect she employs, which in this recording, has been optimised for the surround sound experience. The ability to precisely manipulate fluctuating tempo values within the sequencer also enabled Carlos to produce a convincing performance of the more flexibly interpreted Toccata section.

The famous three short signature flourishes which open the piece are performed using an organ-like timbre (with subtle hints of gamelan). In the Toccata section that follows (from 0:27), the listener is presented with a number of interesting timbres, including metallic sounds and white noise. Also striking is the other-worldly synthetic vocal sound heard between 1:45 and 2:02. Carlos also employs her hocketing technique to great effect throughout this section and places the sounds in a cathedral-like environment. The fugue section, which begins at 2:24, initially emphasises metallic music-box-like tone colours, but later (from 3:49), begins to introduce 'real' instruments, including recognisable sounds of winds and strings, as well as organ-like registrations. Throughout this section, we also encounter some head-swirling spatial effects as different instrumental phrases are batted around the stereo field. The concluding section from 7:14, during which the vocal-like sounds are re-introduced, is quite breathtaking in this regard. Ultimately, the listener is encouraged to simply sit back and bathe in the broad spectrum of tone colours created by Carlos in one of the most evocative and vibrant realisations of Bach in her recorded output.

Tales Of Heaven And Hell (1998)

Personnel:

Wendy Carlos: synthesis, sequencing, performance, arranging, recording and production

Annemarie Franklin: executive producer

Additional musicians:

Jeffrey Johnson, Stephen Rosser, John Olund, Gregory Purnhagen, Ann Feldman: voices

Tom O'Horgan: Live musical instrument and EFX performance

Matthew Davidson: vocal samples and production assistance

Record label: East Side Digital ESD 81352

Format: CD

Recorded at Carlos's Loft studio, Greenwich Village, New York

Release date: 13 October 1998

Highest chart position: US: did not chart

Running time: 57:29

Tales Of Heaven And Hell remains, at the time of writing, Carlos's final unique album release. It did not appear until 1998, six years after *Switched-On Bach 2000,* and was her first recording to be issued by the Minneapolis-based East Side Digital (ESD) label. At the time of completing *Tales Of Heaven And Hell* in 1997, Carlos had not been contracted to a record company for some time. Her last major project with CBS was her collaboration with Al Yankovic on *Peter And The Wolf/Carnival Of The Animals – Part II,* either side of which she had also released recordings with two independent audiophile outfits, Audion (*Beauty In The Beast*) and Telarc (*Switched-On Bach 2000*). Hearing that Carlos was in the market for a contract for her new album, ESD's owner Rob Simonds commented in an interview published in *Billboard* magazine in October 1998: 'That piqued my interest because I am an old fan. I made contact, and when I found out the whole catalogue was available, I got really excited … We've all along kept the focus on progressive music, but this is a fairly significant step forward for us'. Simonds' remarks indicate that ESD's interest was as much about capturing Carlos's recorded legacy as it was in signing an iconic synthesizer artist. Indeed, following the release of *Tales Of Heaven And Hell*, reissuing Carlos's back catalogue became the main priority, the bulk of her work with the label through to 2005 being focused on remastering most of her earlier albums in high definition 'enhanced' CD formats.

    Tales Of Heaven And Hell is, in several respects, a landmark in Carlos's output, conceptually in rather different territory to anything she had done previously. Subtitled 'Musical Drama', this is an album whose material is, like *Digital Moonscapes* and *Beauty In The Beast*, inter-connected by an overarching theme – namely, a musical meditation on the ideas of heaven and hell. An obvious influence on Carlos is late Medieval Catholicism, aspects of which are referenced both in her musical style and in the album imagery. For example, Latin verses (whose texts are provided in the liner notes) form an important part of the musical setting, some of which are spoken, others sung in the style of Gregorian chant. On the CD's back cover, Carlos's album artwork references two iconic paintings by the Netherlandish artist Hieronymus Bosch (c. 1450-1516), arranged in the manner of a two-panel diptych of the type as one might find on a church altar. On the left is an image known as 'Visions Of The Hereafter', which shows a tunnel of light through which angels are conducting souls towards Purgatory, the preliminary stage of cleansing on the journey to Heaven. On the right is a collage of images taken from Bosch's triptych 'The Last Judgment', a disturbing painting which depicts various forms of torture in hell, including impalement on a tree (referred to in Carlos's liner notes as 'Tree Man'). This scene, which brings to mind the depictions of punishment in the famous 'Inferno' section of Dante's *The Divine Comedy*, is evoked vividly in the cries of the damned that permeate the album's extended soundscape composition 'Clockwork Black'. The artwork on the front of the CD also makes specific reference to this track by adapting the classic triangular window which adorned the original Warner Bros *A Clockwork Orange* LP, the eyeball now immersed in hellfire and juxtaposed with the Satanic image of an upside-down crucifix. Beneath this is the disconcerting statement, 'Contains genuinely scary material. Use caution when listening alone or in the dark', a direct reference to the sounds of human suffering in 'Clockwork Black', which makes this the first Carlos album to feature a health warning!

Production-wise, *Tales Of Heaven And Hell* was also Carlos's first project since the score for *Tron* to involve actual musicians in a substantial way. Appearing on the album are a number of vocalists, most notably Jeffrey Johnson and Ann Feldman, both of whom feature prominently on 'Clockwork Black', as well as 'live musical instrument EFX performances' by Tom O'Horgan. At the same time, Carlos's sound remains very much based on the established digital music production practices of the era, including the use of computer sequencing (with her favoured Digital Performer software), synthesis (using a recent Kurzweil model, the K2000) and sampling, marking her full transition into the field of modern music technology. With such refined tools, Carlos also continued to explore her interest in altered tunings – for example, employing what she refers to as 'my own variation on Werkmeister's Circular Tuning' on the track 'Seraphim'. Werkmeister (more usually spelt Werckmeister) tuning dates from the Baroque period and is considered a predecessor to today's widespread equal temperament tuning system. There are also throwbacks to Carlos's analogue past, particularly in her use of the Theremin-like Circon, which she had originally built for use in the soundtrack for *The Shining* (heard on the 'Rocky Mountains' cue). The Circon appears on a number of occasions on the album, where it often has a prominent melodic role, including 'Transitional', 'HeavenScent' and 'Clockwork Black'.

'Transitional' (9:14)

The album begins with the lengthy 'Transitional', which, like many of Carlos's larger compositions, has a complex multi-part structure. As the title suggests, the piece is intended to gradually acclimatise the listener to the sound world of the album, moving by turns between conventional and more abstract musical perspectives, ultimately arriving in a quasi-Medieval soundscape of plainchant. Unusually for Carlos, the piece features a prominent 4/4 drumbeat, punctuated by sampled vocal stabs, whose groove imparts a laid-back 1950s 'lounge music' vibe. Over this vamp, Carlos introduces a simple, attractively shaped melody on the strings, which is subsequently taken up by an accordion-like instrument and woodwinds. After a short rhythmic interlude, the melody reappears on the Circon, whose eerie Theremin-like tone evokes the atmosphere of a horror B-movie. After this, we are in rather different territory: the main beat drops out and the music is more fragmentary in character, with jaunty melodic phrases passed around different instruments, some employing conventional timbres, others decidedly more digital (at 2:56, for example). At 3:28, a march-like beat enters with a swung feel (suggesting an influence of jazz perhaps), ushering in a reprise of the main melody of the first section, again played on the Circon, fragments of which are then uttered by isolated female vocal samples over a bass line intoned by male voices. From 4:39, we are in more abstract 'Timesteps' territory, the music comprising fragmentary interjections of piano melody, percussive sounds and repetitive electronic loops, underlaid by an ominous rhythm on a low muffled bass drum (suggestive of an irregular heartbeat) punctuated by male vocal samples. The accumulated tension of this section eventually gives way to a more peaceful extended passage of wordless chanting by a monks' chorus, which, by the final minute, has evolved into a rich choral tapestry of live and sampled vocal elements.

'HeavenScent' (3:06)

'HeavenScent' is a short, beautiful piece featuring piano and Circon (the latter in a prominent lead role) accompanied by gently undulating strings. The music begins with the piano alone before the Circon enters and doubles its melody, producing a pleasing tonal combination. Carlos suggests in her liner notes that the Circon, with its subtly changing timbre and expressive vibrato, is intended to offer a more 'human' balance to the programmed MIDI aspects of the arrangement (ironic, perhaps, given that this is an electronic instrument). Her performance here brings to mind the artistry of famous exponents of the theremin, such as Clara Rockmore.

'Clockwork Black' (17:47)

The most remarkable piece on the album, 'Clockwork Black' charts a sonic journey into hell, underpinned by key themes from the film *A Clockwork Orange*, which, for Carlos, remain indelibly tainted with the dark subject matter of Kubrick's film. It is a substantial and captivating musical soundscape of nearly 18 minutes in length, whose ambitious scope is comparable to 'Timesteps', the standout composition of the original film soundtrack. In her liner notes, Carlos describes the piece as a 'fantasia on themes from the film score', the word 'fantasia' here implying a loose structure, although the music gains its form to a certain extent from its three vocal texts, which appear at different intervals (one is in English ('Hell Chant'), the other two are in Latin ('Dies Irae' and 'Libera Me')). The main events of the piece are described below:

0:00 – Introduction: the music opens with dissonant, sustained electronic textures and the sounds of distant thunderclaps, setting the scene for hell, followed by ticking clocks (reminding us of 'Timesteps') and clock chimes, which give way to the desperate wailings of the damned. We then hear the first vocal text, 'Hell Chant', with its repeating line 'We are the damned', for which Carlos has chosen to employ a vocoder, an appropriate sonic metaphor for the dehumanised state of hell's victims.

2:23 – We hear the original title music of *A Clockwork Orange*, specifically Purcell's Music For The Funeral Of Queen Mary, first intoned in Gregorian chant style by a monks' choir and then taken up by the Circon.

3:42 – More thunderclaps are followed by a section in which we hear brief snippets of Rossini's 'La Gazza Ladra', a brief reiteration of the 'We are the damned' chant, followed by a full restatement of Music For The Funeral Of Queen Mary, now presented in a similar orchestral guise to its appearance in *A Clockwork Orange* (including the timpani drum rolls and the brief reference to the 'Dies Irae' theme).

6:51 – The Purcell theme is repeated on the Circon and then developed in a gorgeous, almost filmic passage on the lower strings. This gives way to a reintroduction of the clocks and the wailing sounds, over which we hear music from Beethoven's 'Ode To Joy' on the Circon. Another snippet of 'La Gazza Ladra', followed by more thunderclaps, marks a transition to the next section.

9:37 – A melancholy passage in the lower strings, which again draws on the theme of Purcell's Music For The Funeral Of Queen Mary, provides a moment of repose. Purcell's music is then presented in its original guise, the melody first being intoned by the monks over the timpani part before being joined by the brass harmonies. A clock chime signals a sudden explosive electronic effect which darts across the speakers.

12:38 – A solo monk now chants the 'Dies Irae' text, the lines immediately echoed by a sinister whispering voice which ping pongs between the left and right speakers. The Circon then reprises Beethoven's 'Ode To Joy' over a chiming clock as a single voice recites from the final text, 'Libera Me' ('Deliver me'), against a backdrop of insane laughter. A brief snippet of 'La Gazza Ladra' signals the transition to the next section.

14:25 – Clock chimes continue to accompany the increasingly agitated recitation of the 'Libera Me' text. The male speaker appears to become subsumed by the oppressive sonic landscape.

15:10 – Conclusion: A calmer atmosphere. References to the Music For The Funeral Of Queen Mary are heard once again on the strings, eventually morphing into the 'Beethoviana' arrangement heard on the original *A Clockwork Orange* soundtrack. The Circon subsequently joins in the performance of Purcell's theme, providing a highly poignant accompaniment to the pitiful crying (convincingly performed by Ann Feldman), which concludes the piece.

'City Of Temptation' (4:21)

The shorter track which follows 'Clockwork Black' appears on the surface to have an unpredictable structure, in which contrasting musical moods are juxtaposed. However, close listening reveals that the piece is unified by a simple two-note sighing theme which recurs, rondo-like, in different musical guises. The listener is initially situated in a reverberant space and bombarded with thunderclaps and dramatic timpani rolls, implying that we remain within the landscape of 'Clockwork Black'. We then hear an expressive passage in the lower strings outlining the two-note theme, which soon gives way to a quieter passage dominated by a heartbeat rhythm. From 0:58, the theme then reappears as a top-line melody on saxophone (before being passed to other instruments) over an irregular beat in 11/4 time, which Carlos indicates is an influence of Stravinsky's *The Rite Of Spring*. The climactic point of the section occurs at 2:10, the dissonant dramatic music here reminiscent of Carlos's *Tron* style. After a brief interlude, in which the heartbeat rhythm is restated, we return once again to the 11/4 music, now re-orchestrated with chimes. However, this is short-lived and collapses into a brief passage of monks' chanting before we return for the final time to the material of the main theme, now being stated by a brass ensemble, after which the music appears to quickly dissipate.

'Memories' (1:46)

'Memories' provides a brief sentimental interlude, conventionally orchestrated with the familiar tone colours of the LSI Philharmonic. The piece has a simple texture, consisting of a lyrical melody, taken first by the oboe and then flute, over a pulsing string accompaniment in an almost Baroque-like pastiche, which brings to mind Ennio Morricone's composition 'Gabriel's Oboe'. Carlos describes the piece as an 'oasis in the midst of some of my darkest and most pessimistic compositions'.

'Afterlife' (8:24)

Another of the album's more substantial pieces, 'Afterlife' begins in a sinister fashion with sustained synthesizer tones, over which we hear curious bird-like calls reminiscent of Elkind's vocalisations in 'Rocky Mountains'. This turns out to be an atmospheric scene setting which prefaces the introduction of the main motif of the piece: a snaking bass riff which runs continuously through three extended sections of the piece, respectively 0:40-3:47, 4:44-5:55, and finally, from 6:33 to the end. In the manner of a typical blues or jazz piece, this riff provides the harmonic foundation for a series of musical episodes (Carlos's liner notes indicate the form here is a rondo), which present the listener with a number of different instrumental colours and textures. These include a mixed male/female voice choir (with vocal samples), which delivers wordless sustained tones (suggesting an influence of Debussy's 'Sirenes' perhaps), metallic sounds evoking the gamelan of *Beauty In The Beast* and synthetic moaning sounds. There are two obviously contrasting sections, during which the bass riff drops out, the first between 3:49 and 4:43 and the second from 5:56 to 6:32. Both are relatively dramatic in character, featuring more intense vocals, dissonant chords, busy timpani and piercing brass-like stabs. The ending of the track might best be described as the musical analogue of Edvard Munch's painting 'The Scream'!

'Seraphim' (12:49)

The album concludes with 'Seraphim', whose title suggests the angels who guide saved souls to Purgatory in Bosch's 'Visions Of The Hereafter', sentiments which are certainly reflected in this predominantly slow and contemplative piece. Once again, we are presented with an elaborate multi-sectioned composition, beginning with a poignant passage for a small string ensemble and harp, rendered with great realism by Carlos's digital orchestration. The next section features Gregorian chanting (a simple two-part texture with a single voice over a drone) interspersed with decorative flourishes on harp and metallic percussion, which later reappears in a more expansive, reverberant space. Following this, we have a restful instrumental interlude in which short fragments of melody are passed between instruments. These serve to anticipate the music we hear subsequently as Carlos introduces her final Latinate text, entitled 'Antique Antiphony', which is initially presented in a responsorial fashion (that is, one line is intoned by a single voice and then responded to by the group) before becoming more contrapuntal in style. An extended restful orchestral instrumental interlude follows, in which vocal samples are employed as part of the sustained textural backdrop, interjecting occasional phrases of melody. An increasing optimism is apparent in the new theme, which appears at 8:37, pre-empting the final appearance of the Gregorian chant, which now wordlessly intones the music of the 'Antique Antiphony' section. The sublime concluding music (what Carlos calls the 'extended Coda') begins at 10:00 with a beautiful passage for the string quartet before expanding into a fuller string orchestration, which ascends to its final sustained chord.

Miscellaneous, Compilations, Curiosities And Rarities

Electronic Music

Record label: Turnabout TV 4004/TV 3400S
Release date: 1965

Electronic Music showcases the work of a number of composers who, in 1965, were significant names associated with the Columbia-Princeton Electronic Music Center, including Andres Lewin-Richter, Ilhan Mimaroglu and Tzi Avni. The LP gives a sense of where Carlos's musical aesthetic might have headed had she not met Rachel Elkind and been encouraged to explore arranging Bach's music and is also the first example of her electronic music work to appear on record, albeit as part of a compilation. Two Carlos works are featured, her Variations For Flute And Electronic Sound and the Dialogues For Piano And Two Loudspeakers, the latter, it will be recalled, having also been recorded (again with pianist Philip Ramey) for release on *By Request* in 1975 (see the commentary on that album for details). The Variations For Flute And Electronic Sound, a short piece of around four minutes in length, takes a similar approach, marrying live instrumental performance with electronics (the flute part is performed by John Heiss). Carlos's sleeve note indicates that there are six variations in total, the third being entirely electronic and the fourth being more dominated by flute. Variation 2 draws upon canon technique, bringing to mind Bach's compositional style, while the exhilarating Variation 5, in its fast alternation between flute and electronic sound, reminds us of Carlos's later hocketing approach. Overall, it is an accessible and interesting piece whose unusual blend of the acoustic with the synthetic rewards re-listening.

Moog 900 Series Electronic Music Systems Demonstration Record

Record label: R.A. Moog Company, RMD-100
Release date: 1967/1969

The *Moog 900 Series Electronic Music Systems Demonstration Record* is a much sought-after rarity and a genuine curiosity in Carlos's recorded output. It dates from the formative period of her association with Robert Moog when she was mastering the instrument and developing prototype realisations for *Switched-On Bach*. The record is essentially a nine-minute showcase of the sonic possibilities of the Moog 900 Series, narrated by Ed Stokes, designed to market the technology, with its then pioneering voltage control system, as a significant advance on earlier 'classical' electronic studio systems. The listener is educated in the basic elements of electronic music, including waveform types (sine wave, square wave, sawtooth, white noise) and their transformation via voltage control before being treated to a series of synthesizer-generated sound effects, including explosions, wind and cat miaows reminiscent of those used on Carlos's arrangement of 'What's New Pussycat?', the tune of which is also briefly quoted. Further sequences of abstract electronic effects follow, giving way in the last two minutes to music of a more recognisably popular style, clearly intended as a gesture to the traditionally minded listener. A later 1969 release of this disc includes excerpts from *Switched-On Bach*, specifically the Sinfonia To Cantata No. 29 and Brandenburg Concerto No. 3 on its reverse.

Brink Of Death – Single by Childe Harold
'Brink Of Death' b/w 'Anne With Love'

Record label: Limelight 3084
Release date: December 1968

Childe Harold were a short-lived East Coast band formed by singer Bruce Herring in 1967, their style sometimes being referred to (ironically given the Carlos connection) as baroque-pop. 'Brink Of Death', an introspective meditation on dying, was written for the band by Bert Sommer (19491-1990), a singer-songwriter active on the New York scene in the late 1960s/early 1970s, who later starred in the musical *Hair*. The music, which is typical of the folksy psychedelic style of the period, was arranged by Carlos and produced by Elkind (under the TEMPI name), with engineering by Robert Schwartz, indicating that the sessions are likely to have taken place at the city's Gotham Recording Studios. There are several elements that presage Carlos's track 'Timesteps' on *A Clockwork Orange*, including ticking sounds, as well as abstract electronic effects of the *musique concrete* variety, which remind the listener of her earlier experimental work at the Columbia-Princeton Electronic Music Center. Of equal interest is the Byrds-influenced B-side 'Anne With Love', for which Carlos is credited as both composer and arranger. The track's prominent harpsichord part ticks the baroque-pop boxes, as well as bringing to mind Carlos's Bach leanings, while its distinctive synthesizer sounds anticipate her forthcoming electronic classical realisations. Carlos would, of course, have been working on Childe Harold's single around the same time that she was putting the finishing touches to *Switched-On Bach*.

João Gilberto – Album by João Gilberto

Record label: Polydor 2541 037
Release date: 1973

While it might seem strange to include a classic bossa nova album amongst Carlos's recordings, this is an anomaly that deserves the attention of her fanbase. João Gilberto's *João Gilberto*, sometimes referred to as the latter's 'white album', has the distinction of being a Rachel Elkind production, and Carlos's contribution here was as an engineer. The album is of particular interest because it is one of the very few instances of a recording by Carlos which does not involve electronic instruments or synthetic sounds, instead demonstrating her ability to capture superb naturalistic sounding classical guitar, voice and percussion. Only one track on the LP, 'Valsa (Como São Lindos Os Youguis)', breaks with the traditional production mould to give a hint of the creative layering and spatial mixing processes that we encounter in Carlos's synthesizer albums of this period.

Secrets Of Synthesis
Record label: CBS FM 42333/MK 42333, East Side Digital ESD 81702
Release date: 1987/2003

Secrets Of Synthesis, Carlos's final release on CBS Masterworks (in both LP
and CD format), appeared hot on the heels of *Beauty In The Beast* in 1987. It
is a fascinating recording which brings to mind the earlier demonstration LPs
that appeared when electronic music was in its infancy, such as *The Sounds
And Music Of The RCA Electronic Music Synthesizer* (1955) and Beaver and
Krause's *The Nonesuch Guide To Electronic Music* (1968). Carlos's album is an
often revelatory survey (with narration) of the fundamental synthesis, recording
and production techniques employed in her work from *Switched-On Bach* to
Digital Moonscapes, supported by numerous audio excerpts from each of her
albums. Among the topics covered are hocketing, the vocoder, spatial mixing,
alternative tunings, concepts of analogue subtractive synthesis and digital
additive synthesis. As such, this LP provides an excellent, easily understandable
guide to Carlos's development as an electronic musician over the course of her
career and one which can be usefully consulted while exploring her recordings.

Rediscovering Lost Scores, Vols 1 And 2
Record label: East Side Digital ESD 81752/81762
Release date: 2005

Carlos's final ESD release, the two-volume *Rediscovering Lost Scores* set,
brings together a substantial body of her film music composed from the
early 1970s to the late 1990s. A good proportion of this music (split between
the two volumes) comprises the cues Carlos composed for *The Shining*,
the vast majority of which were not used by Kubrick. While much of this
material is difficult to reconcile with the soundtrack that ultimately emerged,
which is now indelibly fused with the film's plot and imagery, it nonetheless
offers insight into how Carlos envisaged a potential score on the basis of
her reading of the Stephen King book. The stylistic range of the musical
material is considerable. 'Colorado', for example, a piece combining a small
orchestra and percussion with Moog, has a dramatic theme reminiscent of
classic Hollywood epic scores of the 1950s. Traditional musical styles are also
apparent in pieces such as 'Chase Music' and 'Nocturnal Valse Triste' – the
latter being one of several tracks to employ the Circon (see also 'Greetings
Ghosties' and 'A Haunted Waltz') – and the sentimental gestures of 'A
Ghost Piano' and 'Paraphrase For 'Cello'. True to Carlos's musical aesthetic,
'Nocturne Valse Triste' is an adaptation of a popular classical piece by
Sibelius, elements of which also run through other cues, such as 'Danny' and
the bizarre 'Subliminal Ballroom'. Another theme that frequently features in
the score, often cleverly re-worked, is the 'Dies Irae', which is the basis of
pieces such as 'A Ghost Piano', 'Fanfare And Drunken 'Dies'', 'Paraphrase
For 'Cello'' and 'Where's Jack?'. Other cues are of a more abstract and
experimental character, closer in style to the music of the final Kubrick score,

including 'Horror Show', a collage of menacing voices, 'Psychic Shout #237' and 'Thought Clusters', both of which depict Danny's telepathic screams through various combinations of orchestral and synthetic timbres. 'Visitors' is a striking textural piece based on a bowed autoharp processed via a vocoder, 'Dark Winds And Rustles' conjures atmospheric, wintry sounds from the Circon, while 'Bumps In The Night', with its use of the recorded sounds of a real party, is in the *musique concrete* vein.

Among the other gems unearthed by Carlos from her earlier film scores are a few unheard cues for *Tron*, including two short alternative versions of the 'Creation Of Tron' theme and 'Lightcycle Games', a piece composed to accompany the famous racing scene but ultimately rejected in favour of sound effects. It is worth noting that the 'special features' disc of the 20th Anniversary Collector's Edition DVD of the film includes a reconstruction of the light cycle sequence with Carlos's original music now added. Finally, there are three additional cues from *A Clockwork Orange*, two of which are variations on Purcell's Music for The Funeral Of Queen Mary, 'Pop Purcell' offering an amusing re-working with a swung feel. The third cue, 'Trumpet Voluntary', is vaguely reminiscent of the fanfare that opens Monteverdi's Orfeo suite on *The Well-Tempered Synthesizer*.

It is the less familiar content of *Rediscovering Lost Scores* that is of particular interest for Carlos fans, namely the collection of seven short soundtracks composed for UNICEF documentary films in the 1970s on Vol. 1 and the partial and complete scores for the films *Split Second* (1992) and *Woundings* (1998) on Vol. 2. The UNICEF scores were created in association with Dick Young Productions, a company that made many documentaries for the United Nations during the 1970s and early 1980s. Carlos and Elkind worked with Young on a number of short films whose subject matter concerns social and cultural life in various Third World locations, including Peru, Ethiopia and Tanzania. As the structure of each score is conceived in relation to the visual imagery, the music often moves abruptly between styles and moods. 'The Children Of Peru', for example, comprises three contrasting pieces, one a dance, the second suggesting a fairground carousel and the third in the character of an instrumental song. This music is widely eclectic, drawing upon classical, popular and 'ethnic' influences, the latter designed to evoke a certain cultural flavour through a combination of instrumental timbres and musical effects, including drones, irregular rhythms, repeating patterns and characteristic scales (see especially 'Daycare And The Colonel', 'Two Distant Walks' and 'Ethiopian Life'). Other tracks, such as the middle section of 'Three Hopeful Places', suggest the influence of European avant-garde classical music. The sound of these recordings also reflects the technological resources regularly employed by Carlos during the 1970s, including her Moog synthesizer and the Yamaha Electone E-5 (acquired around the time of *Switched-On Bach II*). Vocals (presumably Elkind's) also appear on 'Daycare And The Colonel', where they form part of a sustained backdrop.

Split Second is a science fiction horror film released in 1992, a project which experienced a number of ups and downs during shooting, including major script changes and the departure of its original director. The two slight Carlos cues on this album were salvaged from the period of her brief involvement with the film (her music was eventually replaced with a score by Francis Haines and Steve Parsons) and both are tense, brooding numbers, reflecting her well-honed horror composing chops and convincingly rendered using her LSI Philharmonic timbre palette.

Woundings (also known as *Brand New World*) is an independent British anti-war film directed by Roberta Hanley and starring Guy Pearce and Ray Winstone. Carlos states in her liner notes that the score is a collaboration with 'musician friends' Clare Cooper, Manya Zuba and Matthew Davidson, the latter also a contributor to *Tales Of Heaven And Hell*. Unsurprisingly, given that the film was made in the same year, reminiscences of this album are detectable throughout the score. This is clear in the evocative vocal textures of the title music and 'Scattering Ashes' (also bringing to mind 'Incantation' on *Beauty In The Beast*), the archaic stylings of 'Doug Does Angela' and in the instrumental colours of the shorter character cues 'Angela's Walk' and 'Jimmy'. While Carlos has provided detailed explanations of the purposes of each cue in her comments, it is well worth acquiring the film to appreciate the music in its original context.

Finally, *Rediscovering Lost Scores* Vol. 1 includes two tracks composed for Dolby Demonstration films in the early 1980s, one a Bach pastiche, the other an arrangement of Wagner, each offering a brief but delightful reprise of Carlos's 1970s classical music aesthetic.

Carlos Re-Released: The East Side Digital Re-Issues

Between 1998 and 2004, Carlos devoted much of her time to remastering and re-issuing her earlier Columbia, Audion and Telarc recordings in 'enhanced' CD editions for the East Side Digital label. This meant that all her music, with the exception of the *Tron* soundtrack and her collaboration with Al Yankovic *Peter And Wolf/Carnival Of The Animals – Part II*, could now be experienced in much improved high-definition 20-bit audio. Furthermore, all the recordings were re-packaged with extended sleeve notes, featuring, in some cases, new artwork and bonus tracks and including dual CD-ROM encoding, which enabled listeners to gain access to additional information about each album interactively in an offline HTML website format. The East Side Digital re-issues were welcomed by Carlos fans, affording an opportunity to revisit and reflect upon her work in pristine new audio presentations. More importantly, the recordings also rejuvenated her music in the marketplace, making them available to a younger audience who had not known/could not access the long out-of-print LPs. Unfortunately, by 2002, East Side Digital had fallen upon hard times due to the impact of streaming technologies, and with the label's demise in 2009, Carlos's recordings once again became scarce. This, in combination with the unavailability of digital versions of Carlos's music on any online platforms, has naturally driven up CD prices in the second-hand marketplace, where it is not uncommon for them to sell for between £70-£100 per item.

A Clockwork Orange (1998)
Catalogue number: ESD 81362

Carlos's first release on the ESD label was the remastered soundtrack for *A Clockwork Orange* – specifically, the CBS version rather than the Warner Bros film tie-in, which had already been issued three times on CD since the 1980s. The new version includes two short bonus tracks, 'Orange Minuet' and 'Biblical Daydreams', which are here sandwiched between the high-speed electronic version of the William Tell Overture and 'Country Lane'. Like the latter, both were ultimately rejected by Kubrick and were only omitted from the alternative CBS release due to limitations of LP space, likewise affording an opportunity for 'what if?'-style speculation on their potential effect had they been used in the film. 'Orange Minuet' had been composed for the scene in which the results of Alex's behavioural therapy are demonstrated to officialdom in a mock staged performance, Kubrick eventually opting for Terry Tucker's baroque pastiche 'Overture To The Sun' (available on the Warner Bros edition) in the final cut. It is an attractive, tuneful piece which similarly mimics the baroque style, here clothed in synthetic brass tones and accompanied by an appropriately metallic-sounding harpsichord-style continuo part. Carlos intended 'Biblical Daydreams' to conjure up the sequence of images that enter Alex's mind (Christ's Crucifixion, scenes of Roman battle and the harem) as he peruses the bible in the prison library. It is in a more free-form structure, beginning with archaic-sounding music, which then moves briefly into a comedic march-like section before concluding in a gentle series of chords (Carlos states that she also references two vintage songs, 'I Love A Parade' and 'I Want A Girl', during the course of the piece). The album artwork is a re-created image of the original Warner Bros cover, conflated with elements used for *Tales Of Heaven And Hell*, the triangular frame this time featuring Beethoven rather than Alex. Of particular interest is Carlos's additional liner note, which provides valuable information concerning the genesis of the soundtrack and her working relationship with Kubrick.

Sonic Seasonings (1998)
Catalogue number: ESD 81372
The remastered edition of *Sonic Seasonings* contains two previously unissued pieces – 'Aurora Borealis' and 'Midnight Sun' – both of substantial length (each around 20 minutes long), which alone make the 2xCD set well worth acquiring. An additional bonus is a short (c. 5:21) outtake from the fourth movement of the original LP, 'Winter', a sparser track which is missing the wolves and Elkind's vocalisations, hence giving some insight into the music's earlier evolution. 'Aurora Borealis' and 'Midnight Sun' comprise a two-movement suite dating from 1986 entitled *Land Of The Midnight Sun* and are both intended to be musically evocative of the fluctuating play of light on the Northern landscape. The composition and realisation of these pieces are naturally informed by the digital technological perspectives of Carlos's work during this period. In each case, she built up the music layer-by-layer using her Synergy additive synthesizers, improvising musical lines over pre-programmed sequences and overdubbing the music live using a digital recorder, a device which, at the time, did not allow for after-take editing. Both pieces are essentially minimalistic in style, emphasising texture, pattern and chordal character rather than clear-cut melody, and thus, sit well alongside the original *Sonic Seasonings* material. The accompanying CD liner notes include a reflective essay and a brand new set of programme notes that outline the compositional thinking in each piece (in some cases, assuming theoretical knowledge of keys and chords).

Switched-On Boxed Set (1999)
Catalogue number: ESD 81244
Carlos's third ESD reissue focused on the Bach recordings released between 1968 and 1980, which are here re-packaged in a lavish boxed set edition, respectively containing remastered versions of *Switched-On Bach*, *The Well-Tempered Synthesizer*, *Switched-On Bach II* and *Switched-On Brandenburgs*. The first three CDs contain interesting bonus features. On *Switched-On Bach* and *The Well-Tempered Synthesizer*, for example, Carlos provides engaging narrated audio clips of her early recording experiments for each LP. The *Switched-On Bach* CD also includes, as an addendum, the second 1979

realisation of the Adagio movement of Brandenburg No. 3 (first released on *Switched-On Brandenburgs*), which can now be conveniently compared with the original 1968 electronic version. By way of Bach completism, *Switched-On Bach II* inserts the Little Fugue In G Minor (originally released on *By Request*) between the Anna Magdalena pieces and Brandenburg Concerto No. 5. The fourth *Switched-On Brandenburgs* disc (which also contains the 'enhanced' CD data) contains only Concertos 1, 2 and 6 – in other words, it is solely devoted to the new versions which appeared on the LP in 1980. Accompanying the discs are two booklets, one containing the original sleeve notes for each LP, plus a reprint of Glenn Gould's enthusiastic 1968 review of *Switched-On Bach* for *Saturday Night* magazine, the other a more substantial treasure trove of technical information concerning the evolution of Carlos's recording set-up over the years.

Digital Moonscapes (2000)
Catalogue number: ESD 81542
The digitally recorded audio is identical to the original CBS release (which, it will be recalled, was issued on CD as well as LP). On the enhanced CD-ROM, Carlos has supplemented the original (already substantial) liner notes with some additional titbits of information, including a scan of a brochure for the Synergy synth, a 'Moon Facts' chart and a detailed commentary on the rationale behind the completely updated album artwork, which serves to further immerse the listener in the astronomical themes of the recording.

Beauty In The Beast (2000)
Catalogue number: ESD 81552
Another album recorded to an exacting audio standard and previously released on CD, *Beauty In The Beast*'s programme content is here retained as per the original with no additional material. Carlos also (thankfully) retains the original Balinese artwork, which was central to the album's concept, and in particular, its standout extended track 'Poem For Bali'. The original liner notes are slightly expanded with a short interpolated essay entitled 'Looking Back', in which Carlos muses on the pioneering aspects of *Beauty In The Beast*, including the altered tunings, the improvisatory character of the music and its cultural open-mindedness, which she still regards as her most important album.

Switched-On Bach (2001)
Catalogue number: ESD 81602
As the individually packaged remaster of *Switched-On Bach* appeared only two years after the boxed set, the recorded material here is unsurprisingly identical. The accompanying documentation is also very similar, reproducing elements of the text from the aforementioned booklets, including the original liner notes, Carlos's commentaries on the Moog synthesizer and her account of the problematic first album cover (the replacement 'serious'

version now adorns the CD). There is one new item, however – a short but engaging article by Carlos entitled 'A Classic Returns', which reflects on the zeitgeist surrounding the album's emergence in 1968 and also serves as an advertisement for the boxed set.

The Well-Tempered Synthesizer (2001)
Catalogue number: ESD 81612
The individual CD release of *The Well-Tempered Synthesizer* replicates the audio of the boxed set to the letter. In addition to the original liner notes, Carlos has included a new essay entitled 'And For An Encore: (Music As You Like It)', in which she reflects upon the making of the album, noting, in reference to the remastered version, that 'there was nearly as much work expended in restoring the original tracks as in their initial creation.'

Switched-On Bach II (2001)
Catalogue number: ESD 81622
The audio of *Switched-On Bach II* is almost identical to that of the boxed set release. However, Carlos has not included the Little Fugue In G Minor, presumably because she wanted to retain the integrity of the original LP programming for this solo reissue. A welcome addition to the reproduced original liner notes by Robert Moog is a new essay by Carlos entitled 'Déja Vu All Over Again: The Second S-OB Album', which offers an interesting, reflective discussion of the process of creating the LP. Notably, the CD cover is a recreation of the by-then unavailable 'Bach-in-space' image, which adorned the original LP rather than a photographic reproduction.

Switched-On Brandenburgs (2001)
Catalogue number: ESD 81632
The remastered CD release of *Switched-On Brandenburgs* is a double disc set which programmes the Concertos in numerical order (compared to the LP version, which placed Concerto No. 2 on the fourth disc alongside Concerto No. 6). The liner notes reproduce Allan Kozinn's original comments on the history of the Brandenburgs, along with his informative interview with Carlos and Elkind, and conclude with another new reflective essay ('Closure With Style') in which Carlos reflects on the *Switched-On Brandenburgs* period and outlines some of the technical challenges involved in realising Concerto No. 6. The CD cover is a recreation of the image used on the original LP due to the latter's unavailability, Carlos 'fixing several things we hated about the old CBS version' in the process.

By Request (2003)
Catalogue number: ESD 81692
The penultimate album to be remastered for ESD, *By Request*, replicates the original LP programme in its original sequence and has no additional

tracks. This is slightly disappointing, as there was perhaps scope to include previously unheard demo material or tracks that were pressed onto alternative versions of the LP in the aftermath of the copyright issues surrounding Elgar's music in 'Pompous Circumstances'. 'Stay Tuned', for example, which appeared at the end of the Netherlands release, is a curiosity in Carlos's output, which has not seen the light of day since. The enhanced CD component compensates to a degree with its detailed analytical information on the music, particularly 'Pompous Circumstances' (the liner notes also provide an account of its British banning), for which 12 pages of annotated score are provided. *By Request*'s artwork is also new for the release, now showing a close-up of multi-coloured wires protruding from the VCA/Envelope panels of the Moog synthesizer, with each referring to an artist (symbolised as a specific timbre) represented on the album.

Switched-On Bach 2000 (2004)

Catalogue number: ESD 81732

On the 'deluxe new edition', the audio is as per the Telarc release, but the album includes extended liner notes and a new cover that is strongly reminiscent of the original humorous *Switched-On Bach* image that Carlos rejected, the mock-Bach figure now situated in a room that has been furnished with more up-to-date computer technology (together with a replacement cat on the chair to the left).

Bibliography

Anon, 'Col Push On Carlos 'Request'' (*Billboard*, 8 November 1975)

———, 'What's The Strangest Artistic Collaboration You Can Think Of' (*Keyboard*, January 1989)

Clarke, A. C., *2010: Odyssey Two* (Ballantine Books, 1982)

Cooper, K., 'Record Reviews: Switched-On Brandenburgs' (*High Fidelity*, June 1980)

Dilberto, J., 'Wendy Carlos A.D. (After Digital)' (*Downbeat*, March 1987)

Doerschuk, R. L., 'Back To Bach' (*Keyboard*, August 1992)

———, 'Wendy Carlos' (*Keyboard*, September 1992)

———, 'Wendy Carlos: The Magic In The Machine: Reflections From The First Great Modern Synthesist' (*Keyboard*, August 1995)

Ernst, David, *The Evolution Of Electronic Music* (Schirmer Books, 1977)

Fager, C. E., 'Synthetic Sonorities' (*The Christian Century*, 31 December 1969)

Gilbert, J., 'Electronic Music' (*Gramophone*, April 1969)

Glinsky, A., *Switched On: Bob Moog And The Synthesizer Revolution* (Oxford University Press, 2022)

Gould, G., 'The Record Of The Decade' (*Saturday Night*, December 1968)

Greenfield, E., 'Review Of Switched-On Bach II' (*Gramophone*, June 1974)

Armbruster, G. and Darter, T., *The Art Of Electronic Music* (GPI Publications, 1984)

Henahan, D., 'A Tale Of A Man And A Moog' (*The New York Times*, 5 October 1969)

———, 'Switching On To Mock Bach' (*The New York Times*, 3 November 1968)

Hollingworth, R., 'The Walter Carlos Sonic Boom' (*Melody Maker*, 23 September 1972)

Houtkin, A., 'Review Of Beauty In The Beast' (*Computer Music Journal*, Summer 1988)

———, 'Review Of Digital Moonscapes' (*Computer Music Journal*, Spring 1986)

Howe, H. S., 'Recent Recordings Of Electronic Music' (*Perspectives Of New Music*, Spring/Summer 1969)

Lees, G., 'The Electronic Bach: Johann Sebastian Is A Wild, Wild Breakthrough' (*High Fidelity*, December 1968)

LoBrutto, V., *Stanley Kubrick: A Biography* (D.I. Fine Books, 1997)

L.S., 'Review Of The Well-Tempered Synthesizer' (*Gramophone*, March 1970)

Marcus, L., "Son Of Switched-On Bach': Or What Went Wrong In The Delivery Room' (*High Fidelity*, February 1970)

Milano, D., 'Wendy Carlos' (*Contemporary Keyboard*, December 1979)

———, 'Wendy Carlos: Defying Conventions, Discovering New Worlds', (*Keyboard*, November 1986)

Moog, R., 'Wendy Carlos And Michael Fremer Reveal The Secrets Behind The Soundtrack Of TRON' (*Keyboard*, November 1982)

Morris, C., 'Wendy Carlos Takes Her Moog Music To East Side Digital' (*Billboard*, 3 October 1998)

P.K., 'Review Of Sonic Seasonings' (*Stereo Review*, September 1972)

Salzman, E., 'Moog Moosic' (*Stereo Review*, January 1969)

Schonberg, H. C., 'A Merry Time With The Moog?' (*New York Times*, 16 February 1969)

Sewell, A., *Wendy Carlos: A Biography* (Oxford University Press, 2020)

Somerville Mann, W., 'Review Of Sonic Seasonings' (*Gramophone*, February 1973)

Tatnall Canby, E., 'Review Of Digital Moonscapes' (*Audio*, October 1985)

Trocco, F., and T. J. Pinch, *Analog Days: The Invention And Impact Of The Moog Synthesizer* (Harvard University Press, 2004)

Walker, A., *Stanley Kubrick Directs* (Harcourt Brace Jovanovich, 1972)

'Wendy Carlos HomePage' *https://www.wendycarlos.com/*

On Track Series

Allman Brothers Band – Andrew Wild 978-1-78952-252-5

Tori Amos – Lisa Torem 978-1-78952-142-9

Aphex Twin – Beau Waddell 978-1-78952-267-9

Asia – Peter Braidis 978-1-78952-099-6

Badfinger – Robert Day-Webb 978-1-878952-176-4

Barclay James Harvest – Keith And Monica Domone 978-1-78952-067-5

Beck – Arthur Lizie 978-1-78952-258-7

The Beatles – Andrew Wild 978-1-78952-009-5

The Beatles Solo 1969-1980 – Andrew Wild 978-1-78952-030-9

Blue Oyster Cult – Jacob Holm-Lupo 978-1-78952-007-1

Blur – Matt Bishop 978-178952-164-1

Marc Bolan And T.rex – Peter Gallagher 978-1-78952-124-5

Kate Bush – Bill Thomas 978-1-78952-097-2

Camel – Hamish Kuzminski 978-1-78952-040-8

Captain Beefheart – Opher Goodwin 978-1-78952-235-8

Caravan – Andy Boot 978-1-78952-127-6

Cardiacs – Eric Benac 978-1-78952-131-3

Nick Cave And The Bad Seeds – Dominic Sanderson 978-1-78952-240-2

Eric Clapton Solo – Andrew Wild 978-1-78952-141-2

The Clash – Nick Assirati 978-1-78952-077-4

Elvis Costello And The Attractions – Georg Purvis 978-1-78952-129-0

Crosby, Stills & Nash – Andrew Wild 978-1-78952-039-2

Creedence Clearwater Revival – Tony Thompson 978-178952-237-2

The Damned – Morgan Brown 978-1-78952-136-8

Deep Purple And Rainbow 1968-79 – Steve Pilkington 978-1-78952-002-6

Dire Straits – Andrew Wild 978-1-78952-044-6

The Doors – Tony Thompson 978-1-78952-137-5

Dream Theater – Jordan Blum 978-1-78952-050-7

Eagles – John Van Der Kiste 978-1-78952-260-0

Earth, Wind And Fire – Bud Wilkins 978-1-78952-272-3

Electric Light Orchestra – Barry Delve 978-1-78952-152-8

Emerson Lake And Palmer – Mike Goode 978-1-78952-000-2

Fairport Convention – Kevan Furbank 978-1-78952-051-4

Peter Gabriel – Graeme Scarfe 978-1-78952-138-2

Genesis – Stuart Macfarlane 978-1-78952-005-7

Gentle Giant – Gary Steel 978-1-78952-058-3

Gong – Kevan Furbank 978-1-78952-082-8

Green Day – William E. Spevack 978-1-78952-261-7

Hall And Oates – Ian Abrahams 978-1-78952-167-2

Hawkwind – Duncan Harris 978-1-78952-052-1

Peter Hammill – Richard Rees Jones 978-1-78952-163-4

Roy Harper – Opher Goodwin 978-1-78952-130-6

Jimi Hendrix – Emma Stott 978-1-78952-175-7
The Hollies – Andrew Darlington 978-1-78952-159-7
Horslips – Richard James 978-1-78952-263-1
The Human League And The Sheffield Scene –
Andrew Darlington 978-1-78952-186-3
The Incredible String Band – Tim Moon 978-1-78952-107-8
Iron Maiden – Steve Pilkington 978-1-78952-061-3
Joe Jackson – Richard James 978-1-78952-189-4
Jefferson Airplane – Richard Butterworth 978-1-78952-143-6
Jethro Tull – Jordan Blum 978-1-78952-016-3
Elton John In The 1970s – Peter Kearns 978-1-78952-034-7
Billy Joel – Lisa Torem 978-1-78952-183-2
Judas Priest – John Tucker 978-1-78952-018-7
Kansas – Kevin Cummings 978-1-78952-057-6
The Kinks – Martin Hutchinson 978-1-78952-172-6
Korn – Matt Karpe 978-1-78952-153-5
Led Zeppelin – Steve Pilkington 978-1-78952-151-1
Level 42 – Matt Philips 978-1-78952-102-3
Little Feat – Georg Purvis - 978-1-78952-168-9
Aimee Mann – Jez Rowden 978-1-78952-036-1
Joni Mitchell – Peter Kearns 978-1-78952-081-1
The Moody Blues – Geoffrey Feakes 978-1-78952-042-2
Motorhead – Duncan Harris 978-1-78952-173-3
Nektar – Scott Meze – 978-1-78952-257-0
New Order – Dennis Remmer – 978-1-78952-249-5
Nightwish – Simon Mcmurdo – 978-1-78952-270-9
Laura Nyro – Philip Ward 978-1-78952-182-5
Mike Oldfield – Ryan Yard 978-1-78952-060-6
Opeth – Jordan Blum 978-1-78-952-166-5
Pearl Jam – Ben L. Connor 978-1-78952-188-7
Tom Petty – Richard James 978-1-78952-128-3
Pink Floyd – Richard Butterworth 978-1-78952-242-6
The Police – Pete Braidis 978-1-78952-158-0
Porcupine Tree – Nick Holmes 978-1-78952-144-3
Queen – Andrew Wild 978-1-78952-003-3
Radiohead – William Allen 978-1-78952-149-8
Rancid – Paul Matts 989-1-78952-187-0
Renaissance – David Detmer 978-1-78952-062-0
Reo Speedwagon – Jim Romag 978-1-78952-262-4
The Rolling Stones 1963-80 – Steve Pilkington 978-1-78952-017-0
The Smiths And Morrissey – Tommy Gunnarsson 978-1-78952-140-5
Spirit – Rev. Keith A. Gordon – 978-1-78952- 248-8
Stackridge – Alan Draper 978-1-78952-232-7

Also available from Sonicbond

Status Quo The Frantic Four Years – Richard James 978-1-78952-160-3
Steely Dan – Jez Rowden 978-1-78952-043-9
Steve Hackett – Geoffrey Feakes 978-1-78952-098-9
Tears For Fears – Paul Clark - 978-178952-238-9
Thin Lizzy – Graeme Stroud 978-1-78952-064-4
Tool – Matt Karpe 978-1-78952-234-1
Toto – Jacob Holm-Lupo 978-1-78952-019-4
U2 – Eoghan Lyng 978-1-78952-078-1
Ufo – Richard James 978-1-78952-073-6
Van Der Graaf Generator – Dan Coffey 978-1-78952-031-6
Van Halen – Morgan Brown – 9781-78952-256-3
The Who – Geoffrey Feakes 978-1-78952-076-7
Roy Wood And The Move – James R Turner 978-1-78952-008-8
Yes – Stephen Lambe 978-1-78952-001-9
Frank Zappa 1966 To 1979 – Eric Benac 978-1-78952-033-0
Warren Zevon – Peter Gallagher 978-1-78952-170-2
10cc – Peter Kearns 978-1-78952-054-5

Decades Series
The Bee Gees In The 1960s – Andrew Mon Hughes Et Al 978-1-78952-148-1
The Bee Gees In The 1970s – Andrew Mon Hughes Et Al 978-1-78952-179-5
Black Sabbath In The 1970s – Chris Sutton 978-1-78952-171-9
Britpop – Peter Richard Adams And Matt Pooler 978-1-78952-169-6
Phil Collins In The 1980s – Andrew Wild 978-1-78952-185-6
Alice Cooper In The 1970s – Chris Sutton 978-1-78952-104-7
Alice Cooper In The 1980s – Chris Sutton 978-1-78952-259-4
Curved Air In The 1970s – Laura Shenton 978-1-78952-069-9
Donovan In The 1960s – Jeff Fitzgerald 978-1-78952-233-4
Bob Dylan In The 1980s – Don Klees 978-1-78952-157-3
Brian Eno In The 1970s – Gary Parsons 978-1-78952-239-6
Faith No More In The 1990s – Matt Karpe 978-1-78952-250-1
Fleetwood Mac In The 1970s – Andrew Wild 978-1-78952-105-4
Fleetwood Mac In The 1980s – Don Klees 978-178952-254-9
Focus In The 1970s – Stephen Lambe 978-1-78952-079-8
Free And Bad Company In The 1970s – John Van Der Kiste 978-1-78952-178-8
Genesis In The 1970s – Bill Thomas 978178952-146-7
George Harrison In The 1970s – Eoghan Lyng 978-1-78952-174-0
Kiss In The 1970s – Peter Gallagher 978-1-78952-246-4
Manfred Mann's Earth Band In The 1970s – John Van Der Kiste
978178952-243-3
Marillion In The 1980s – Nathaniel Webb 978-1-78952-065-1
Van Morrison In The 1970s – Peter Childs - 978-1-78952-241-9
Mott The Hoople And Ian Hunter In The 1970s –

Also available from Sonicbond

John Van Der Kiste 978-1-78-952-162-7
Pink Floyd In The 1970s – Georg Purvis 978-1-78952-072-9
Suzi Quatro In The 1970s – Darren Johnson 978-1-78952-236-5
Queen In The 1970s – James Griffiths 978-1-78952-265-5
Roxy Music In The 1970s – Dave Thompson 978-1-78952-180-1
Slade In The 1970s – Darren Johnson 978-1-78952-268-6
Status Quo In The 1980s – Greg Harper 978-1-78952-244-0
Tangerine Dream In The 1970s – Stephen Palmer 978-1-78952-161-0
The Sweet In The 1970s – Darren Johnson 978-1-78952-139-9
Uriah Heep In The 1970s – Steve Pilkington 978-1-78952-103-0
Van Der Graaf Generator In The 1970s – Steve Pilkington 978-1-78952-245-7
Rick Wakeman In The 1970s – Geoffrey Feakes 978-1-78952-264-8
Yes In The 1980s – Stephen Lambe With David Watkinson 978-1-78952-125-2

On Screen Series
Carry On... – Stephen Lambe 978-1-78952-004-0
David Cronenberg – Patrick Chapman 978-1-78952-071-2
Doctor Who: The David Tennant Years – Jamie Hailstone 978-1-78952-066-8
James Bond – Andrew Wild 978-1-78952-010-1
Monty Python – Steve Pilkington 978-1-78952-047-7
Seinfeld Seasons 1 To 5 – Stephen Lambe 978-1-78952-012-5

Other Books
1967: A Year In Psychedelic Rock 978-1-78952-155-9
1970: A Year In Rock – John Van Der Kiste 978-1-78952-147-4
1973: The Golden Year Of Progressive Rock 978-1-78952-165-8
Babysitting A Band On The Rocks – G.d. Praetorius 978-1-78952-106-1
Eric Clapton Sessions – Andrew Wild 978-1-78952-177-1
Derek Taylor: For Your Radioactive Children –
Andrew Darlington 978-1-78952-038-5
The Golden Road: The Recording History Of The Grateful Dead – John Kilbride 978-1-78952-156-6
Iggy And The Stooges On Stage 1967-1974 – Per Nilsen 978-1-78952-101-6
Jon Anderson And The Warriors – The Road To Yes –
David Watkinson 978-1-78952-059-0
Magic: The David Paton Story – David Paton 978-1-78952-266-2
Misty: The Music Of Johnny Mathis – Jakob Baekgaard 978-1-78952-247-1
Nu Metal: A Definitive Guide – Matt Karpe 978-1-78952-063-7
Tommy Bolin: In And Out Of Deep Purple – Laura Shenton 978-1-78952-070-5
Maximum Darkness – Deke Leonard 978-1-78952-048-4
The Twang Dynasty – Deke Leonard 978-1-78952-049-1

And Many More To Come!

Would you like to write for Sonicbond Publishing?

At Sonicbond Publishing we are always on the look-out for authors, particularly for our two main series:

On Track. Mixing fact with in depth analysis, the On Track series examines the work of a particular musical artist or group. All genres are considered from easy listening and jazz to 60s soul to 90s pop, via rock and metal.

On Screen. This series looks at the world of film and television. Subjects considered include directors, actors and writers, as well as entire television and film series. As with the On Track series, we balance fact with analysis.

While professional writing experience would, of course, be an advantage the most important qualification is to have real enthusiasm and knowledge of your subject. First-time authors are welcomed, but the ability to write well in English is essential.

Sonicbond Publishing has distribution throughout Europe and North America, and all books are also published in E-book form. Authors will be paid a royalty based on sales of their book.

Further details are available from www.sonicbondpublishing.co.uk. To contact us, complete the contact form there or
email info@sonicbondpublishing.co.uk